Paul's Letters

For Today's Christian

REV. PAUL A. FEIDER

Foreword by Eugene LaVerdiere

TWENTY-THIRD PUBLICATIONS
P.O. Box 180 Mystic, CT 06355

Dedication

To Mom and Dad
–in Christ,
for the gift of
life,
love,
and the name I bear.

 ISBN 0-89622-154-7.

Library of Congress Catalog Card No. 81-86678

Edited by Amy Burman
Designed by John G. van Bemmel
Cover by Robert Maitland

FOREWORD

Saul-Paul, the apostle to the Gentiles, was a single-minded man, completely at the service of the gospel. In his preaching, which took him to most of the great cities of the Greco-Roman world, he boldly presented the death and resurrection of Christ as the source of salvation for all peoples.

Paul's message, spoken with the power of the Spirit and shared with the dedication of the cross, held little room for indifference. Like Christ crucified whom he preached, Paul himself was a stumbling block to Jews, an absurd little man to the Gentiles, but a powerful expression of God's wisdom for all who were called in Christ (see 1 Corinthians 1:23-24).

The spirit of Paul reaches across the ages through the tradition of life and commitment that focused his energies and touched his hearers. His message lives in the letters he wrote, which the early Christians lovingly collected and included in what eventually became our New Testament. Like Paul himself, these letters have always been at the center of controversy, and this simple fact is the finest witness to their authenticity.

The controversies are of various kinds. Some reflect the struggle to understand a message spoken long ago in another language, a message shaped by other cultures and addressing the problems of young communities in a world that did not share their values. Other controversies stem from appeals to Paul as an authority in conflicts that divided the church at various times in its history. Still others emerge from the Christian effort to receive and live Paul's message unselfishly in the evangelizing mission of the church: How can we become pauline Christians today? This last kind of controversy is nothing other than the interior dispute that every serious Christian has with what Paul called the flesh.

Paul Feider's guide to Paul's letters falls into this last category. On the surface, the book does not appear controversial. However, as we slowly read its simple and illuminating text, we soon find ourselves fighting the many resistances that hold us back from Christian living.

Introductions, commentaries, and guides do not all have the same purpose. Some are written so that the reader may understand what Paul was saying. They do not necessarily require that the readers align themselves with the readers Paul himself had in mind. Such commentaries may serve a Christian purpose, but they are not inherently Christian. They might even be written by one who is altogether foreign to Paul's gospel experience and convictions.

Other commentaries and guides are intrinsically Christian. Their aim is to enable the letters to fulfill their purpose, that is, to shape and stimulate the Christian life of the reader. They are intended for Christians who want to live as Paul lived, in the service of the gospel. The writer of such a guide can only be a friend of Paul, one who has journeyed on Paul's way, who resonates with the spirit of the apostle, and who has personally felt the challenging impact of his message. Paul Feider's guide is of this second kind.

A Christian guide such as this is extremely important for the church. Humble and self-effacing, it plays the role of Timothy, Titus, and others, Paul's associates who bore his letters to the communities, presented them, helped the readers to taste Paul's word, and added pertinent observations to facilitate comprehension and acceptance.

May this book move all of us to a similar service and to extend Paul's mission to the ends of the earth.

Eugene A. LaVerdiere, S.S.S.
Catholic Theological Union
Chicago, November 3, 1981

PREFACE

Over the years many people have asked me what they might read or study to help them understand the bible. I rejoiced to hear people thirsting to know God's word, yet I realized that many of the theology books we use to deepen our knowledge of scripture were too complex and advanced for "regular people," ordinary people to understand. In an attempt to respond to these people and many others who are seeking to deepen their understanding and appreciation of God's holy word, I wrote this simple guide to the letters of Saint Paul. Paul's works are worth the effort of study because they deal with very practical, down-to-earth situations that are part of living a Christian life. In addition, his life-witness of Jesus as Lord can enrich our faith journey.

In this guide, I use the tools of scripture scholarship and my own experience to help give a feel for the context in which Paul's letters are written and read. Just as all of our words are spoken in a specific situation, and most easily understood in that context, so too with God's word. The more we can hear and feel God's message in the historical setting in which it was spoken, the more accurately and richly we can apply it to our own lives. To take any words out of context, whether someone else's or God's, does a disservice to the one who spoke them.

This guide deals with the thirteen letters most commonly attributed to the authorship of Saint Paul. (Scholars are quite certain that Paul wrote the Letters to Thessalonians, Galatians, Philippians, Corinthians, Romans and Philemon. Some scholars question whether Paul personally wrote the Letters to Colossians, Ephesians, Timothy, and Titus. We will examine their reasoning when we get to those letters.)

The questions included within these pages are meant to help draw us personally into the scripture verses. They may also be used as guides for initiating group discussion.

Let me add that any journey into God's word must be accompanied by prayer. We must come to the Author of life himself and ask him to open our hearts and minds to the meaning of his message for our lives. This book is only a tool to help that prayer be fulfilled.

I hope this journey into the writings of Paul will help us deepen our appreciation of the beautiful message God left us in those letters.

Contents

NOTE OF THANKS

I wish to express my gratitude
– to those who through their instruction
have helped me understand and appreciate
God's precious word,
– to those who by their life-witness
demonstrate that God's word
is alive today,
– to those in the St. Thomas More community
who participated in bringing this book
to completion.

I give thanks to my God every time
I think of you – which is constantly,
in every prayer I utter – rejoicing, as
I plead on your behalf, at the way you
have all continually helped promote the
gospel. . . .

Philippians 1:3-5

INTRODUCTION TO SAINT PAUL

Any time we study scripture, we become aware of the fact that God's word is alive. It has power to touch and change that part of every human person that knows when the creator speaks. People who search to hear and understand God's message in scripture will discover that transforming and guiding power. As we embark on this journey into the writings of Saint Paul, we open ourselves to hear God's word within our own lives and the life of our community.

In studying the bible, we become very aware that God always speaks his word to people in a particular setting within their own culture, their own educational background, their own life, just as he speaks to us in ways we can understand. To fully appreciate the power of his message, it is important to get a feel for the context or the situation in which his word was heard and written. To best hear God's message to us through Paul's writings, we will take a moment to explore Paul's life, personality, and theology. This will help us put into context the word God speaks through him.

The Life of Paul

According to Acts of the Apostles and his own letters, Paul was an energetic, powerful, loving person. He was born in Tarsus in Cilicia of Jewish parents and became a good Jew educated in Jewish Law. If we could sit and talk with him, Paul probably would tell us that his "real birth" was that day on his way to Damascus when he was struck down with the realization that by persecuting the Christians he was persecuting Jesus the Lord (read Acts 9:1-19, Acts 22:1-21, or Acts 26:4-23). This event, recounted three times in Acts of the Apostles and alluded to in Paul's letters, was the central experience of his life: the beginning of a whole new way of life. He says he experienced the risen Lord. This realization that Jesus was the son of God, and that he was alive, changed Paul's life and compelled him to tell others that real life meant accepting Jesus as Lord. Paul's letters indicate that he proclaimed the message of Jesus wherever he traveled.

Paul's life gives evidence that he himself is an epistle; he is a living letter. He was completely transformed by Jesus Christ and his life witness enfleshed the power of Jesus' resurrection.

There is no known date of Paul's birth. His conversion on the road to Damascus was the day he started "living." From all that can be uncovered, that event probably occurred around the year A.D. 36. All of the dates of his life are scholarly estimations because events were not documented then as they are today.

Paul's knowledge of the Greek language and his understanding of people outside of Judaism, together with his education in Jewish thought, gave him the necessary tools to bring the early Christian message to the Gentiles. The fact that he took the Jewish message from Jerusalem and made it understandable to non-Jewish people – the Gentiles – and brought it all the way over to Rome, has had a profound effect on the history of Western civilization. Some authors say that next to Jesus, Paul has had the greatest impact on religious thinking in the Western world. God chose a fitting instrument to spread his message, and Paul's acceptance of God's choice made him a significant person. As we come to know Paul through his letters, we will begin to see what made him so effective.

The main events of Paul's life after his conversion center around his three missionary journeys to cities and regions along the northern coast of the Mediterranean Sea, and around his trip to Rome. (See map on page 144.) An overall view of those journeys and the letters he wrote along the way may give us some insight as to why he addressed this or that issue in a particular epistle. The following is the most commonly accepted outline of the events of Paul's life. The dates are approximate.

A.D. 36 Conversion

46-49 *First Missionary Journey*

Beginning in Antioch, Paul and Barnabas traveled to Cyprus, Perga, Antioch, Iconium, Lystra, Derbe, Galatia, and back to Antioch (Acts 13:1-14:28). Following that journey they went to Jerusalem to meet with the apostles and presbyters for a council (Acts 15:1-35).

49-52 *Second Missionary Journey*

Beginning in Antioch, Paul and Silas traveled through the regions of Syria, Cilicia, Galatia, to the city of Troas. From Troas they went to Philippi, Thessalonica, Beroea, Athens, and Corinth, where he wrote his letters to the *Thessalonians.* They then went on to Ephesus, Caesarea, and back to Antioch (Acts 15:40-18:22). During this journey, Paul started many Christian communities in Greece.

54-58 *Third Missionary Journey*

Beginning in Antioch, Paul revisited communities in Galatia, Phrygia, and Ephesus, where it seems he wrote to the *Galatians, Philippians,* and *Corinthians.* Then he traveled through Philippi and Thessalonica to Corinth, where he wrote to the *Romans.* After his stay, he returned to Jerusalem by way of Philippi, Troas, Miletus, and Caesarea (Acts 18:23-21:19). Paul was imprisoned by the Jews after arriving in Jerusalem and eventually was taken to Rome for trial.

61-63 Paul was put under house arrest in Rome. Here it seems he wrote his epistle to *Philemon,* to the *Colossians,* and to the *Ephesians.*

65-67 For a time before his death, Paul was imprisoned in Rome, where he probably wrote to his disciples *Timothy* and *Titus.*

67 Paul was martyred.

Throughout his travels, Paul started Christian communities that lived on the power of Jesus' message. On occasion he found reason to write to those communities to encourage them, to admonish them, or to address some of the problems that arose. The words of Jesus are heard through Paul's writings as he witnesses to his own relationship with the Lord and shares his understanding of how Jesus' teachings apply to specific situations. By studying Paul's letters in the historical order in which they were written (as close as we can determine that order), we will be able to see him grow in his knowledge and love of Jesus. The more we put ourselves in the context of these letters, the more we will hear God speak to our hearts through them.

The Theology of Paul

In addition to knowing Paul's background, we may also enrich our understanding of his letters and God's message in them by getting an overall view of the way Paul explains things: his theology. Paul came to know Jesus in a very personal way on the road to Damascus, and so his proclamation of the Good News strongly emphasized the transforming power of a personal relationship with Jesus. Paul knew that power firsthand. His life and writings are taken up with bringing others to know the power of Jesus' resurrection.

Somewhere in Paul's experience of Jesus and coming to know the Father, he realized that the Lord he knew from his Jewish heritage, Yahweh, was the same Abba, father of Jesus. He saw a unity in salvation history there. Paul experienced Jesus on the road, and then experienced the Father as the same Lord God that the Jewish people worshipped. Paul discovered and proclaimed all of salvation history as one process of God's love for his people, with Jesus as the fulfillment and culmination of all known history.

He believed that God chose the Jewish people to play a significant role in his plan of salvation, but because some of them did not accept Jesus as the son of God and redeemer, God allowed the Gentiles to experience the saving effects of Jesus' death and resurrection. With this universal vision of salvation, Paul challenged the early church to accept and preach to *all* people.

As part of his universal vision of God's saving plan, Paul came to understand and proclaim the centrality of Jesus

Christ in that plan. More than anyone of his time, he discovered and put into words the redeeming and reconciling effects of Jesus' death and resurrection. His letters are saturated with the message that real life begins with accepting Jesus as Lord.

Questions for Reflection and Discussion

1. In seeking to understand Paul's writings, what facts about his life seem most significant?

2. How did Paul know Jesus personally?

3. Have you ever had an experience similar to Paul's on the road to Damascus?

4. Do you feel you know Jesus personally? If so, how do you experience his presence day-to-day?

5. In what ways can knowing the context of God's word help us understand it today?

6. Has anyone ever taken your words out of context? How did it make you feel?

Chapter 1

The First Letter to the Thessalonians

Father, we gather here in your name because you have chosen us and called us – each in our own way – to spread your good tidings to those around us, to our families, and to the many people we meet along life's journey. May the sharing that we do inspire us and enrich us in our relationship with you. May our look at Saint Paul help us to be an example and a witness to your life in us. This we ask through Christ our Lord. Amen.

The First Letter to the Thessalonians is the first of Paul's letters. It is written in Corinth about the year A.D. 51. We get a picture of a young, fervent Christian community, a community existing about twenty years after the resurrection of Jesus.

Read 1 Thessalonians 1:1
Paul will begin all of his letters with a beautiful greeting like that.

Read 1 Thessalonians 1:2-4
A number of things begin to surface here. We see how grateful Paul is for this community. Gradually, we will come to feel Paul's deep love for all the Christian groups he started. It's amazing that he could be so caring for all the different nationalities within these groups. Remember that most of these communities were mixtures of peoples, Jews and Gentiles, from all over the known world. He accepted them all.

What types of people do you find the hardest to accept? How can you grow in accepting them?

____

____

Read 1 Thessalonians 1:5
If anyone teaches us that there is power in the word, Paul does it. He knows, and has seen with his own eyes, that God's word is more than just any word. God's word changes people's lives.

Read 1 Thessalonians 1:6
Paul experienced the power of God at his conversion and gradually came to understand the transforming power of God's Holy Spirit. The more he traveled and proclaimed the message of Jesus, the more he came to realize that that same power was transforming the lives of many people. This living presence of God is what he called the Holy Spirit.

How do you experience the power of the Holy Spirit?

____

____

Read 1 Thessalonians 1:7
The community of Thessalonica had become a model for all of Greece. The loving witness of the community became known all around the regions of Macedonia and Achaia in Greece.

Read 1 Thessalonians 1:8-10
We see how the community witness to the changed lives of "regular people" was very important in the early church. What spread the gospel message was the fact that many people reformed their lives and became, like Jesus, more sensitive to the needs of people.

In what ways have you seen the powerful effects of your life witness, or the life witness of someone else?

____

____

Read 1 Thessalonians 2:1-4
Some time after Paul left the community of Thessalonica, Jews came in and tried to convince the people that Paul was not a real apostle, that he was a fake. Paul wrote to the community of Thessalonica to reassure them that he had not come to them out of selfish motives or trickery, but out of love for them.

What motives cause you to do the things you do? Are your motives ever misunderstood?

____

____

These next verses point out why Paul had such a profound effect on people.

Read 1 Thessalonians 2:5-12
Paul had a great love for the people in the communities that he started. If we do not feel the love that Paul has for these people, we will not understand the words he says to them. We know that we can only challenge people we really love. When Paul starts exhorting these people or when he calls them to reform, we know that he is speaking out of love for them. Paul loves his people "as a father does his children," and it is through that love that they come to experience the love of God, their Father.

Think of the times you have been healed through the deep love of another person. What effects did that healing love have on your life?

____

____

Read 1 Thessalonians 2:13
Paul did not want to proclaim his own word; he wanted to be very sure to proclaim the word of God. He believed that the word of God was alive and active, that it had a transforming effect on those who allowed it to touch them. Each of the communities was visible evidence of that.

Read 1 Thessalonians 2:14-20
Paul speaks here about the suffering inflicted upon himself and the community by some of the Jews. The Jews chased Paul, put him in prison, and even stoned him to make him stop preaching Jesus' message of salvation to the Gentiles. Jews even attempted to confuse or break up the Christian communities Paul had started. From Acts 13:45 we get the impression that jealousy was the root of their hostility. We rejoice at Paul's perseverance, for mainly through his efforts, the early church came to realize that Jesus' saving death and resurrection were not only for Jews, but for Gentiles as well.

How persevering are you when you know you are following God's call?

____

____

Read 1 Thessalonians 3:1-5
Paul explains why he sent Timothy, his helper, to the Thessalonian community. Paul is always very encouraging to his communities.

Read 1 Thessalonians 3:6-13

Paul is overwhelmed with joy to hear that his community is doing well. He loves his people dearly; that love was the most powerful tool of his ministry.

What do you find is the most powerful tool of your ministry?

___

___

Read 1 Thessalonians 4:1-12

Paul reminds the Christian community that they must live differently than the Gentiles in their neighborhoods who did not know God. The moral lives of the pagan Gentiles at this time were probably quite free, to say the least. Paul's instructions "from the Lord Jesus" call people to change their behavior, which, as we know, is not always easy. Paul exhorts them to control their desires and refrain from cheating. It would be their unselfish love and concern for others that would give "good example to outsiders" and allow them to experience the refreshing Spirit of peace that comes from living in Christ.

Do you think it was harder for these people to live Jesus' values than it is for us? Why or why not?

___

___

Read 1 Thessalonians 4:13-17

Who would be raised from the dead at Jesus' second coming seems to be the main concern of this letter. Knowing some background of these verses may help us understand them. When Paul founded the Thessalonian community early in his ministry, he believed that the second coming of Jesus, which is called the Parousia, was going to occur very soon. In fact, when he was in Thessalonica, he thought it would be coming before any more people died. Since then, he had traveled down to Corinth, and as time passed, people in the community of Thessalonica died. The friends and relatives of the dead were grieved, thinking that those who had died before Jesus' second coming would not share in the resurrection.

Read verses 13-17 again.
Paul's response to this concern not only gave hope to the surviving relatives, but proclaimed Jesus' promise of resurrection for all of us. We can console one another with this message. At the time Paul wrote this letter (c. A.D. 51) he continued to believe that Christ would be returning soon. We can tell from his letters that as time went on he became less and less concerned about the second coming of Jesus. The more he came to understand and appreciate the Spirit of Jesus already present and active in the world, the less he awaited a "second coming." The more we can experience and be aware of Christ present in our everyday lives, the less we have to worry about his second coming.

Read 1 Thessalonians 5:1-6
The Thessalonians were wondering exactly when Jesus would return a second time. Paul indicates that it may be sudden, but, as for when, he does not know. Recall that Jesus himself said that only the Father knows. Paul wants his people to be ready to meet Jesus by "putting on faith and love."

How can we be attentive to the Lord coming into our lives each day?

____

____

Read 1 Thessalonians 5:7-10
Here Paul uses a bit of imagery. He wants his people to be protected by the virtues of faith, love, and hope.

Read 1 Thessalonians 5:11-19
Paul encourages the community to keep up the good work and gives them some instructions for Christian conduct. He is direct and precise in his teachings. He calls for a constant openness to God's will, a constant talking to him in prayer, and allowing his Spirit to work in every part of our lives.

In what ways do you feel the Spirit of God helping you do the things Paul mentions in these verses?

____

____

Read 1 Thessalonians 5:20-22
From the beginning of his teachings, Paul encouraged people to be open to the promptings of the Spirit and to test those promptings within the Christian community, the church. Together, as one community, the early church discerned God's message for his people.

Which people in your Christian community help you hear and discern God's Spirit in your life?

____

____

Read 1 Thessalonians 5:23-28
Paul ends his letter with a prayer of blessing for the people he loves.

Summary Questions

1. What do you believe is the main message of the First Letter to the Thessalonians?

____

____

2. What do you hear God saying to you through this letter?

____

____

Questions for Reflection and Discussion

1. What do you believe is the main message of the First Letter to the Thessalonians?

2. What do you hear God saying to you through this letter?

3. What types of people do you find the hardest to accept? How can you grow in accepting them?

4. How do you experience the power of the Holy Spirit?

5. In what ways have you seen the powerful effects of your life witness, or the life witness of someone else?

6. What motives cause you to do the things you do? Are your motives ever misunderstood?

7. Think of the times you have been healed through the deep love of another person. What effects did that healing have on your life?

8. How persevering are you when you know you are following God's call?

9. What do you find is the most powerful tool of your ministry?

10. Do you think it was harder for these people to live Jesus' values than it is for us? Why or why not?

11. How can we be attentive to the Lord coming into our lives each day?

12. In what ways do you feel the Spirit of God helping you do the things Paul mentions in 1 Thessalonians 5:11-19?

13. Which people in your Christian community help you hear and discern God's Spirit in your life?

Chapter 2

THE SECOND LETTER TO THE THESSALONIANS

Father, we are grateful for the life we have been given through you. Like Saint Paul, we would like to make our whole life a life with you. May our study of your word strengthen us and refresh us in the presence of your spirit. Help us to draw closer to you and to form communities where the atmosphere of your love will lead others to know your deep love for them. This we ask through the power of your Spirit, abiding in us now and forever. Amen.

As far as we can tell, the Second Letter to the Thessalonians was written about the same time as, or recently after, Paul's first letter to them. Paul wrote this letter around the year A.D. 51, from Corinth, after he had visited the community at Thessalonica. It seems Paul's main purpose for this letter was to clarify some questions arising again in the community about the second coming of Jesus. He also used this occasion to encourage the Thessalonian community to persevere under their persecution.

Read 2 Thessalonians 1:1-2
Paul, together with his disciples Silvanus and Timothy, again greets the community in the name of the Lord.

Read 2 Thessalonians 1:3-4
Here we recapture Paul's great love and care for his people. He also reemphasizes the importance of their witness in proclaiming the message of Jesus Christ. Paul is reassuring to them and tells them they are doing a good job. He has a way of encouraging people that makes them want to keep up their good work.

What people in your life encourage you in that way?

____

____

Read 2 Thessalonians 1:5-10
Paul encourages the Thessalonians to persist in their courage against the persecution by the Jews. He expresses his conviction that on the day of Christ's second coming, which he expected very soon, those who were inflicting the persecution would get their just punishment.

Read 2 Thessalonians 1:11-12
Paul prays for his people often and cares for them with deep love. He wants them to become all that God created them to be.

Do you pray often for the people in your care?

____

____

Read 2 Thessalonians 2:1-3a
In his first letter, Paul tried to clear up some concerns about the second coming of Jesus. From these verses, we get the impression that after he wrote his first letter, certain dishonest people started false rumors and wrote false letters, confusing

the members of the community. You can understand why Paul becomes angry. People were writing letters to the Thessalonian community telling them that the day of the Lord had already come, and then signing Paul's name. You can imagine how confusing it could be for people if various "proclaimed leaders" were teaching conflicting things. Paul asks the community to trust him because his teaching was in union with the total Christian Church. He does not know how or when Jesus will return, but he puts people at peace in the knowledge that if they live in Christ, they will share in his final resurrection.

How do you distinguish trustworthy teaching from false or questionable teaching?

____

____

Read 2 Thessalonians 2:3b-12

In this section, Paul describes in apocalyptic language his understanding of how Christ will finally annihilate all evil. Terms like "mass apostasy" and "man of lawlessness" are taken from apocalyptic literature, which uses imagery to describe the struggle between the forces of good and evil. At this point in history, apocalyptic thought bore witness to the belief that a certain force was going to take over the world but something restrained it. From Paul's description, we cannot tell exactly what or who this restraining force was. At one point in the original Greek text, he refers to this restraining force as a "him," suggesting it to be masculine; in the next line he uses the pronoun "it," suggesting it to be neuter. Perhaps Paul was not clear as to the exact nature of this restraining force. From his description, we get the impression that Paul believes that this lawless one sounds somewhat like Satan, but Paul never equates the two. The lawless one would be let loose when the day of the Lord came. The lawless one was to rule for a time and then be destroyed by the presence of the Lord Jesus. Paul is very aware of the power of Jesus' resurrection. He tells those who "open their hearts" to the truth of Jesus' victory over death that they need not fear. As time goes on, Paul will more and more stress the power of living in the Lord's presence, and say less and less about Christ's second coming.

What do you think causes people today to be more concerned about the second coming of Jesus than about his ongoing presence already in their midst?

____

____

Read 2 Thessalonians 2:13-14
Having dealt with the issue of the second coming, Paul again affirms the members of the community. Paul has a beautiful way of making people feel special in God's eyes, as indeed we all are.

Read Thessalonians 2:15-17
Paul encourages his people to stand firm in what he taught them, that Jesus died and rose so that *all* might be free. To all who open their hearts to this message of God's love, there is "eternal consolation" and renewed strength.

In what ways do you express this consoling and affirming message of God's love to others?

____

____

Read 2 Thessalonians 3:1-5
Paul pleads with the people to pray for him as he goes about his difficult mission. He would not be asking these people to continually pray for him if he did not believe in the power of prayer. Very early in our Christian tradition, people believed in and experienced the effectiveness of prayer. The early eucharistic worship services had a specified time during which people would pray for one another's needs.

During your private and communal prayer, do you take time to pray for others?

____

____

Read 2 Thessalonians 3:6
Paul did not want his people to become confused again by those who were teaching falsely. He tells the members of the community to avoid them.

Read 2 Thessalonians 3:7-9
Paul worked as a tentmaker so that he would not have to receive money from the community. Paul could have accepted money, but he wanted to speak of the need for work by his example of work. As we come to know Paul better, we will see that his whole life, especially his relationship with Jesus, is a powerful witness. His life is his best epistle. When we are able to teach others by simply saying "imitate me," we have become a good Christian teacher. This is Paul's method, and his communities are evidence of its effectiveness.

Who are some other people who have taught with their lives?

____

____

Read 2 Thessalonians 3:10-13
Some people in the community stopped working because they believed that the Lord was coming very soon. After all, why plant the crops if no one will be around to harvest them? Paul "urges them strongly in the Lord Jesus" to start working again that all might have food to eat. His corrective words are expressed firmly yet gently.

To what situations might these verses apply today?

____

____

Read 2 Thessalonians 3:14-15
The early church struggled with finding a way to correct members of the community who were doing wrong. Recall at that time, and perhaps even today, the main way of spreading the gospel was the good "life witness" of the members. Paul suggests here a way of lovingly calling people to follow the rule of the community. In cases where a person's bad conduct caused public scandal and seriously harmed the community witness, he recommended more severe treatment, although always with the hope of bringing the offender to final salvation in Christ.

How does the church today seek a balance between calling its members to correction and ministering the forgiving love of Jesus?

____

____

Read 2 Thessalonians 3:16-18
Paul ends his second letter with a blessing. He has one more contact with his Thessalonian community after this letter.

Summary Question

What facet of Jesus' message comes across the strongest to you through this letter?

____

____

Questions for Reflection and Discussion

1. What facet of Jesus' message comes across the strongest to you through this letter?

2. What people in your life encourage you as Paul does in 2 Thessalonians 1:3-4?

3. Do you pray often for the people in your care?

4. How do you distinguish trustworthy teaching from false or questionable teaching?

5. What do you think causes people today to be more concerned about the second coming of Jesus than about his ongoing presence already in their midst?

6. In what ways do you express this consoling and affirming message of God's love to others?

7. During your private and communal prayer, do you take time to pray for others?

8. Besides Paul, who are some other people who have taught with their lives?

9. To what situations might 2 Thessalonians 3:10-13 apply today?

10. How does the church today seek a balance between calling its members to correction and ministering the forgiving love of Jesus?

Chapter 3

The Letter to the Galatians

Father, we give you thanks and praise for the life we can live with you through Jesus, your son. Through the study of this letter, help us to deepen our faith in your plan of salvation. Renew in us an awareness of the power of Jesus' death and resurrection. Keep us fervent in our commitment to your will so that the fruits of your Spirit will grow in our lives. May your name be glorified forever and ever. Amen.

Paul wrote to the Christian communities in the region of Galatia in approximately A.D. 54. At this time, he was beginning his third missionary journey and had just finished visiting the Galatian communities. After leaving them, it seems he received news that some false teachers had come and had attempted to confuse the people regarding their salvation in Jesus Christ. Also, the false teachers accused Paul of not being a true apostle. It is from that context that Paul wrote to the Galatians. We can understand why this letter was written with so much feeling. Paul loved the people of his community and he was very angry with those who were teaching them false doctrines. In passionate eloquence, Paul silences the false teachers. He justifies his claim as an apostle and then develops his teaching on the nature of justification in Jesus Christ.

How do you respond when you find people in your care being adversely influenced by others?

____

____

Read Galatians 1:1-2
In his opening line, Paul declares his apostleship based on his personal calling by Jesus Christ. He refers here to his experience of the risen Christ on the road to Damascus. Paul knew Christ. He felt sent or "apostled" by him to proclaim the good news.

Read Galatians 1:3-5
Paul has a beautiful way of capturing the whole message of salvation in one sentence – and praising God for it besides!

Read Galatians 1:6-7
Paul moves right to the issue that was burning in his heart. He is disappointed that the Galatians have so quickly turned away and listened to someone else. Paul is gentle with his people, perhaps realizing that, as new members of the faith, it is difficult for them to discern the true message of Christ. He will not be as gentle in his words to the false teachers.

Read Galatians 1:8-9
A little of Paul's humanity comes through as he expresses his anger. He truly cares for the welfare of his people.

Read Galatians 1:10-12
Paul expresses his deep commitment to Christ and his desire to serve him. He is hurt that people undermined his preaching. In a few brief statements, he makes it clear that his calling came from Christ and was not for personal gain. There is something very powerful about these lines. Paul is sharing the very core of his Christian commitment with the Galatians. His words challenge us to review our motives and to rededicate ourselves to serving Christ.

How can you identify with Paul's feelings expressed in these verses?

____

____

Read Galatians 1:13-16

This is the first place in his letters where Paul talks about his earlier life and how he persecuted the early church. (See Philippians 3:6; 1 Corinthians 15:9.) Paul gives us the impression that he always did things with extreme zeal and much pride. He was probably one of the most prominent of those persecuting the Christians, and he probably knew Jewish law better than most of his contemporaries. It was amazing, even to him, how God could choose such a person to proclaim the gospel. In awe and gratitude, Paul speaks of God's favor. Since the day he met the Lord on the road to Damascus, he gradually came to realize that God had been acting in his life since before birth, forming him into an instrument to reveal the message of salvation.

Do you ever take time to reflect on how God has been acting in your life?

____

____

Read Galatians 1:17-2:9

Paul describes some of the events since his conversion to show the Galatians that he is a true apostle. In verse two, he indicates his desire to have his teaching in union with the leaders of the church. Consequently, he submits his understanding of the gospel message to them for review. Paul deeply senses the need for a unified Christian message. Some of his pride shows through when the leaders have nothing to add to what he is telling the Gentiles. His acceptance and affirmation by the leaders in Jerusalem renews his strength in resisting the false teachers who tried to undermine his teaching. Paul loves his people and he makes sure that he is instructing them in the truth.

What means can we use to ensure that our teachings are true and faithful to Christ's message?

___

___

Read Galatians 2:10
Even before the church leaders had asked for money for the poor in Jerusalem, Paul was already making efforts to help them. He took up a collection among the communities he established and brought it to the poor in Jerusalem. Eventually, such collections became a symbol of unity within the church. Paul played a significant role in promoting unity among the various Christian communities. This unity was based on Christ and was expressed in sound teaching and concern for the needy.

In what ways do you show your concern for the poor?

___

___

Read Galatians 2:11-14
A little background will help us understand the importance of the incident described in these verses. In Paul's home community at Antioch, the Christians had appeased most of the old hostilities between Jews and Gentiles because they believed all people were one in Christ. Peter had come to visit the community and had eaten with Jewish and Gentile Christians alike, for he was convinced that all were saved through Jesus. (See Acts 10:24-48 and Acts 15:7-12.) When James' group, which

was still very strict in its observance of Jewish regulations, came to Antioch, Peter bowed to peer pressure and stopped eating with the Christian Gentiles. With brilliant courage, Paul addresses the issue immediately because it stands at the core of his conviction that all are saved and washed clean through their faith commitment to Jesus Christ. Basically, Paul told Peter and all those present that in Christ they had to accept one another as brothers and sisters. The old Jewish regulations no longer applied. All were now one in Christ. As we will see in the following verses, Paul uses this story to get to the point of his letter to the Galatians.

How do we sometimes pressure one another into being exclusive either socially or religiously?

____

____

Read Galatians 2:15-21

These verses represent one of Paul's central teachings to the Galatians and to the whole early Church. Paul points out that a person does not have to become a Jew in order to become a Christian. He proclaims that people are not justified by observance of the Jewish laws but by faith in Jesus Christ.

It will be helpful to define what Paul means by justification and how it differs from salvation. Paul uses the word justification to mean being made righteous with God, to be in right relationship with him. This is accomplished through a faith relationship with Jesus. Salvation, as Paul uses it, refers to that final union that Christians hope one day to share with the Lord. In simple words, justification refers to what is already, while salvation refers to what has not yet happened.

Read Galatians 2:15-21 again

Paul tells the Galatians that it is through Jesus that they receive the gift of being made right with God. Their new life with God comes not through the law, but through Jesus. Although they have been justified through Jesus' death and resurrection, they are not free to sin. Only through a life lived in Christ, "crucified to him," can they hope to arrive at eternal salvation.

In what ways do you express your gratitude for God's gift of justification?

____

____

Read Galatians 3:1-5
Paul's deepest feelings emerge from these lines. He must have been disappointed that the community strayed from his teaching so quickly. They had forgotten the wonders God had worked in their midst. With undying persistence, Paul again tells the people how they can share in the freeing power of God's Spirit.

What are some wonders in your life that you may have forgotten?

____

____

Read Galatians 3:6-25
In these verses, Paul uses the example of Abraham to show how justification comes through faith in God. In verse 19 and following, he goes on to give his understanding of Jewish law. In his words, "the law was our monitor until Christ came to bring about our justification through faith." Paul tries very hard to bring people to live in the freedom of Christ's redeeming grace.

Read Galatians 3:26-4:7
Paul expresses the positive aspects of being justified with God. He speaks of the new unity and feeling of familiarity that people can experience as one in Christ. The community at Anti-

och was evidence of that. He also points out that those justified receive a new status as children of God able to speak of God as Abba, meaning "father" or even "daddy." Because Paul had come to feel the power and freedom of being a son of God, he very much wanted his people to know that same experience.

How can you bring other people to experience God as Abba?

____

____

Read Galatians 4:8-11
Lest all his efforts be wasted, Paul encourages the Galatians not to enslave themselves again to Jewish law.

Read Galatians 4:12-20
Paul becomes intimate with the Galatians. He expresses his gratitude to them for accepting him just as he was when he came to them, but he is hurt at their change of spirit. It is beautiful to see how dearly he loves his people, even referring to them as his children.

Which people in your life have loved you to the extent of genuinely hurting for you?

____

____

Read Galatians 4:21-31
Using the story of Abraham and his two sons, Paul proclaims the freedom found in Christ.

Read Galatians 5:1-12
The false teachers who came into the Galatian community after Paul had left were telling people that circumcision was necessary to be right with God. Paul clearly points out the false-

ness of that instruction, and then in true sarcasm, expresses his anger at those who were teaching it (verse 12). Paul has patience with those who were seeking the Lord, but he has no kind words for those who were unsettling and misleading his people.

Read Galatians 5:13-15
Paul addresses himself to the issue of how a Christian should live. Up to this point, Paul has emphasized that people are justified by faith. Now he goes one step further by saying that being made right with God (justification) will only lead to eternal life with him (salvation) if a person follows Christ's law of love. Our freedom as children of God calls us to "place ourselves at one another's service." Paul tells the Galatians that they are free from the regulations of Jewish law, but that they must act according to Jesus' law of love. In the following verses, Paul goes on to say that Christ empowers us through his Spirit to live his way.

How do you feel the Lord is calling you to live out his law of love in your life?

____

____

Read Galatians 5:16-26
Paul explains human temptations as the flesh warring against the spirit, almost as a constant battle within us. He encourages people not to yield to the cravings of the flesh, but to live by the Spirit. The power to do this comes from Christ's resurrection, which is at work in all who believe in him. In verse 22, Paul beautifully summarizes the fruits of God's Spirit, the attitudes that should radiate forth from the life of a Christian. The manifestation of these fruits in one's life is the clearest sign that a person is living in the power of God's Spirit and is on the road to salvation.

How do you discern the workings of God's Spirit in your life?

____

____

Read Galatians 6:1-10
In these few verses, Paul instructs the Galatians in community life. He tells them to deal with sinners gently and to "carry one another's burdens." His instructions are very straightforward and down to earth.

To what situations in your life can you apply this message?

____

____

Read Galatians 6:11-18
As Paul concludes his letter, he makes sure that the Galatians notice that it is written in his own handwriting. He does not want them to be led astray again. He reemphasizes the importance of being "created anew" through the cross of Jesus Christ. As before, Paul ends his letter with a blessing.

In this letter, Paul has shared his heart and soul with the Galatians and with us. It seems evident that he would give anything to bring his people to know the saving power of Jesus Christ, and his letter encourages us to do the same.

Summary Question

What messages do you hear the Lord saying to you through this letter?

____

____

Questions for Reflection and Discussion

1. What messages do you hear the Lord saying to you through this letter?

2. How can you identify with Paul's feelings expressed in Galatians 1:10-12?

3. Do you ever take time to reflect on how God has been acting in your life?

4. What means can we use to ensure that our teachings are true and faithful to Christ's message?

5. In what ways do you show your concern for the poor?

6. How do we sometimes pressure one another into being exclusive either socially or religiously?

7. In what ways do you express your gratitude for God's gift of justification?

8. What are some wonders in your life that you may have forgotten?

9. How can you bring other people to experience God as Abba?

10. Which people in your life have loved you to the extent of genuinely hurting for you?

11. How do you feel the Lord is calling you to live out his law of love in your life?

12. How do you discern the workings of God's Spirit in your life?

13. To what situations in your life can you apply this message?

Chapter 4

The Letter to the Philippians

God our Father, you continually speak your words of love to us. We are grateful that you spoke the word, your son, into our midst. He accepted the humility of death by crucifixion that we might be raised to true and eternal life with you. Empower us to take on his attitude and accept your will for our lives. May all that we are and all that we do proclaim him as Lord, that together with him our whole being might be a hymn to your glory forever and ever. Amen.

The Letter to the Philippians is the warmest and most intimate of all Paul's letters. The Christian community at Philippi was very good to Paul, supporting him with their gifts and their love. He writes to thank them for their support and to warn them against the false teachers who were constantly trying to undo his work of ministry.

Philippi was a Roman city of northern Greece. During Paul's second missionary journey (c. A.D. 50), he formed a Christian community there. He now writes to them from prison (1:13-14). Most data indicate that this letter was written about A.D. 56, during Paul's imprisonment in Ephesus. Certain abrupt transitions within the letter (2:19, 3:2, and 4:10) lead some scholars to believe that the Letter to the Philippians may be a composite of several letters written to the community around this time. Whatever the exact makeup, this letter is truly a love letter in which Paul shares his affection for his people and his deep faith in Jesus Christ. His witness of the power flowing from Christ's resurrection would be a source of encouragement and strength for the Philippians and all who proclaimed Jesus as Lord.

Read Philippians 1:1-2
Paul greets the community at Philippi proclaiming their holiness. Note that even "regular people" can be holy. He then makes a reference to bishops and deacons among them. This brief reference seems to indicate that Paul set up guardians and assistants to care for the community after he left. This practice became the pattern for establishing pastoral leadership among Gentile communities in the early church. We will see more of this in Paul's letter to Timothy and Titus.

Read Philippians 1:3-11
In these verses, Paul expresses a very warm word of thanks for the support he received from the Philippian community during his imprisonment. He allows us to know the joy he felt in thinking about the Philippians. They were "dear" to him and he appreciated their support. The power of Christian fellowship is evident here. He longed to be with them and in a very concrete way through their support and love, he was. He loved them with the affection of Christ and prayed that their life journey would lead to final salvation in Christ, to the glory and praise of God. What a beautiful hymn of gratitude and love! What a powerful prayer for the fullness of life!

For which people in your life might you pray as Paul does in these verses?

____

____

Read Philippians 1:12-18
These verses reveal a strong sense of optimism in Paul. Although he is in prison, his entire attention is focused on how

Christ is being proclaimed. He rejoices at the witness value of his "chains." Because he is so pleased that the word of God is being "fearlessly spoken," he does not seem to be disturbed by the ulterior motives with which it is being done.

How might we draw encouragement from these verses?

____

____

Read Philippians 1:19-26
Paul again conveys his gratitude for the prayers and support of the Philippians. He is confident that his imprisonment will lead to his ultimate salvation and the glory of Christ. In that assurance, he ponders the value of life in this world in relation to eternal life with Christ. His faith is amazingly strong and his selflessness is clearly evident. He is completely surrendered to God's will. Because he believes it would be more beneficial to his people if he were to remain alive, he is confident that the Lord will not allow his imprisonment to end in death.

How do you think Paul grew to become so confident in his faith that real life meant living in Christ?

____

____

Read Philippians 1:27-30
In these verses, Paul exhorts the community members to continue in their good conduct and their unity of purpose. Some "opponents" had confused and disunited his communities in Galatia and Paul did not want the same thing to happen to the Philippians. He reminds them to remain one in the Lord. In union with the Lord, Paul says they are "privileged" to suffer with him. The early church spoke of the privilege of suffering

with Christ, but there must have been days when even Paul did not experience his suffering as a "privilege." His words here, however, do indicate his powerful vision and understanding of being united with Christ. In his Second Letter to the Corinthians, he will further express his way of seeing redemptive value in the sufferings inherent in living the Christian life.

In what ways have you ever seen or experienced the power of a unified Christian witness?

____

____

Read Philippians 2:1-5
Paul affectionately appeals to the Philippians to continue living in harmony with an attitude of humility. His words are powerfully simple. The Philippians' harmony will last if they constantly look to others' interests rather than their own. Briefly, he sums up what should be the attitude of all Christians: they must imitate Christ. Paul draws upon an early Christian hymn to communicate exactly what he meant.

Read Philippians 2:6-11
This hymn, which Paul uses to express the attitude of Jesus, contains probably the richest teaching about Christ found in the entire New Testament. In poetic form, it captures a profound understanding of God expressed in Jesus Christ. Let us discover its richness as God's word. The hymn begins by describing the preexistence of Jesus. Even before he came to earth, Jesus was one with God-Father. In emptying himself, Jesus did not empty himself of his divinity, only of the status of glory to which he had a right as God. He became human like us, experiencing all the normal human realities of life without special privileges. He lowered himself even further by accepting the humblest death, death on a cross. Because of this – because he obediently accepted the Father's will – God highly exalted him and restored him to his former status of glory giving him the name Lord, a name reserved for God alone. Out of

reverence for his saving action, everyone would come to adore him as God and proclaim that he is Lord. The pattern of Jesus emptying himself and humbly accepting the Father's will was to be the pattern for every Christian's life. This precious hymn deepens our appreciation of Jesus' life and captures for all of us the way to eternal life with God.

What parts of this hymn make you feel closer to Jesus and deepen your love for him?

____

____

Read Philippians 2:12-18

Paul urges the Philippians to continue their selflessness as they work toward salvation in Christ. With God's help, he says, they will continue to beget good fruit. Using the image of shining stars, he assures them of the value of their life-witness. Paul is both happy and proud that his community is doing well. He is ready to accept even death if he must, knowing that his efforts in Philippi have been fruitful.

Read Philippians 2:19-3:1

These verses express Paul's love for his co-workers. Timothy was like a son to him. Apparently, he had helped Paul establish the Philippian community. Paul has hopes of sending him to care for the needs of the people whom he so loved. Epaphroditus, another assistant, took the gift from the Philippians to Paul in prison at Ephesus, but then became very sick. Paul recognizes God's hand in his recovery and urges the community to welcome him back in love. Verse one of Chapter 3 can be understood as part of a farewell from Paul, which leads some scholars to believe that verses 2:19-3:1 were originally part of another letter. In any case, it is addressed to the Philippian community and it certainly is done in both the style and love of Paul.

Read Philippians 3:2-11

In referring to pagans, Jews used the term "unbelieving dogs." Ironically, Paul uses that same term here to refer to those Judaizers or false teachers who came into his communities and tried to disturb his people. The term is not particularly complimentary, but then Paul probably has some recent memories of what these people did among his Galatian communities. As he mentions here, they attempted to convince the Christians that it was necessary to observe old Jewish rituals in order to be saved. Paul had been a Pharisee and consequently knew Jewish legal observances. He makes it clear that he has come "to rate all those things as rubbish" in light of the surpassing knowledge of Christ. As he told the Galatians, so now he tells the Philippians that his justification is found not in Jewish law, but through faith in Jesus Christ. Paul wants to know the "power flowing from Christ's resurrection" because he is aware that this is essential in his life if he is to arrive at eternal salvation. These verses are a powerful witness of how Jesus changed Paul's life. He can change the life of anyone who allows him to do so.

In what ways have you felt the power of the risen Lord change your life?

____

____

Read Philippians 3:12-16

In these verses, Paul explains that transformation of one's life takes time. Even after many years, he is aware that the Lord is not finished with him yet. Paul does indicate, however, that he has allowed Christ to "grasp" his whole being, which allows the process to continue. No matter what stage people are at in their Christian journey, Paul accepts them and encourages them to go on. He is very tolerant of anyone who is trying. His words are very meaningful, especially for those called to lead others in Christian growth.

How does Paul's witness speak to you as you journey toward salvation?

____

____

Read Philippians 3:17-4:3

Having given his own testimony, Paul now tells the Philippians to imitate him. He does not want them to get mixed up with those who are set upon things of this world. Paul explains that real and eternal life is in the heavenly realm. Because he loves his people very much, he urges them to stand firm in the Lord. He then pleads for reconciliation between two women who apparently had a disagreement. Paul wants the community to live in harmony.

Read Philippians 4:4-9

Paul knows the power of a unified witness and he hopes that the community at Philippi will be a model of real joy and unselfishness for non-Christians. He wants the Philippians to be free of all anxiety by trusting totally in God's care. If they live according to what he has taught them in Christ, he is confident that they will know the peace that comes only from God. In these few verses, Paul leaves an encouraging message for all Christian communities.

How does your Christian community express some or all of the attitudes mentioned in these verses?

____

____

Read Philippians 4:10-23

As a conclusion to his letter, Paul thanks the Philippians for their constant generosity. They support him in his work more than any other community. We see why Paul holds them "dear." He had not sought any gifts from them, but he accepts their generosity as a sign of their deep love and concern for him. Their love strengthens him to minister to others. Paul is aware that they need to embrace each other with the strength of Christ. In him they have strength for everything. In conclusion, he prays that God will continue to supply all their needs. He closes the letter with his usual greeting and blessing.

In what ways do you feel strengthened by the love someone has for you?

____

____

In the Letter to the Philippians, Paul leaves us a rich message about Christ and his power to change the lives of all who accept his love. God's transforming love is evident in Paul and within the community. Love begets love, and the depth of relationship between Paul and the Philippian community strengthened both of them to bear fruit in Jesus' name.

Summary Questions

How do you feel after reading Paul's letter to the Philippian community?

____

____

What impresses you the most about Paul?

____

____

Questions for Reflection and Discussion

1. How do you feel after reading Paul's letter to the Philippian community?

2. What impresses you the most about Paul?

3. For which people in your life might you pray as Paul does in Philippians 1:3-11?

4. How might we draw encouragement from Philippians 1:12-18?

5. How do you think Paul grew to become so confident in his faith that real life meant living in Christ?

6. In what ways have you ever seen or experienced the power of a unified Christian witness?

7. What parts of this hymn make you feel closer to Jesus and deepen your love for him?

8. In what ways have you felt the power of the risen Lord change your life?

9. How does Paul's witness speak to you as you journey toward salvation?

10. How does your Christian community express some or all of the attitudes mentioned in Philippians 4:4-9?

11. In what ways do you feel strengthened by the love someone has for you?

Chapter 5

The First Letter to the Corinthians

Father, we praise you and bless you because we know that each of us has been favored by you. Each of us has been anointed by your Spirit. As we open ourselves to your word, renew us in the knowledge that you care for us and that you love us. Fill us with the desire to use all the gifts of your spirit to give honor to you. We make our prayer in the name of Christ your Son who gives us life now and forever. Amen.

To better understand Paul's letters to the Corinthian community, we might recall that Corinth was a port city on the Mediterranean Sea and one of the centers of trade. The city was cosmopolitan, made up of people from almost everywhere in the known world. Even though people there had committed themselves to Christ and formed a community, it would take time for them to transform old habits and truly be molded into one people. Paul has patience with them.

When we look at 1 Corinthians, we usually think that this is the first letter that Paul wrote to the Corinthian community. Actually, Paul seems to have written at least four letters to them. From various references, it appears that the second and fourth letters were preserved for us. In 1 Corinthians 5:9, Paul refers to a former letter that was apparently lost, and in 2 Corinthians 2:4 and 7:8, he describes what seems to be another missing letter. References such as these make us aware that God's word, as found in Scripture, is the preservation of precious pieces of manuscripts.

1 Corinthians, as we know it, was written about A.D. 57 from Ephesus. Paul established this Corinthian community around A.D. 50 and lived there a year and a half. He knew and loved the people there. Paul had heard disquieting news about some quarreling going on in the Corinthian community. He writes them a long letter addressing numerous issues, such as factions in the community, sexual immorality, use of charisms, and questions about resurrection. We will probably be able to find ourselves between the lines of this letter more than others, because Paul deals with the kinds of issues that still challenge Christian communities today.

What do you see as significant issues within Christian communities today?

____

____

Read 1 Corinthians 1:1-3
Paul has such a powerful way of greeting the community and affirming them in the Lord. He makes us feel "consecrated in Christ" just by reading his words.

Read 1 Corinthians 1:4-9
With gentle care, Paul expresses his gratitude to God for these people. For someone who has heard unsettling news about the Corinthian community, Paul comes across strongly affirming and caring. That is what makes Paul Paul. He knew the healing power of genuine love.

Can you recall an incident in which you expressed gentle love at a time when anger may have been expected?

____

____

Read 1 Corinthians 1:10-13
Paul is saddened by the news of factions forming in the community. He is aware that these people come from many backgrounds. He lovingly calls them to unity explaining that there is only one baptism in Christ.

How might you apply this message to Christian communities today?

____

____

Read 1 Corinthians 1:14-16
Here is a brief indication that Paul himself did not perform many baptisms. His calling was to preach the gospel. We presume his helpers did the actual baptizing. Verse 16 is one of the few references in the New Testament where we see a whole household being baptized (see Acts 16:33). In the early church, the whole family was baptized on the basis of the parents' faith.

Read 1 Corinthians 1:17-25
This next section on wisdom might make more sense if we recall that Corinth is in Greece. In Greece, the philosophers would stand on the street corners, attract a group of disciples, and talk philosophy, exchanging words of wisdom. You will remember when Paul was in Athens, he tried to compete with these people on a philosophical level. It simply didn't work. The message of Christ does not fit with an exchange of worldly wisdom. In these verses, Paul eloquently tells the Corinthians and us that God's wisdom is far beyond human wisdom. Paul uses the terminology of the people to enlighten them in God's

wisdom. He shows how God has gone beyond the Jews' demand for signs and the Greeks' demand for wisdom by calling all of them to believe in the saving death and resurrection of Christ. Paul has a deep appreciation of God's ways.

Read 1 Corinthians 1:26-31
We see from these verses that the Corinthian community was made up of "regular people." However, God made them "special" through his calling, and as such, they had reason to boast.

In what ways can you identify with the Corinthians?

____

____

Read 1 Corinthians 2:1-16
Paul tells the people that as a human being he had real fears. From personal experience he had become very aware of his need for the strength and courage of God's Spirit. Paul knows that it is the Spirit of God who endows faith-filled people with the gifts they need. In verse after verse, Paul is praising God for his magnificent, generous ways.

Read 1 Corinthians 3:1-9
In the simple imagery of feeding infants, Paul indicates his patience and gentleness with the newborn Christians. He knows that growth takes time. His example of the growing seed speaks profoundly of his awareness that God is the source of life. He was teaching his people, as co-workers, to recognize the real "author of life."

What do these two images say to you?

____

____

Read 1 Corinthians 3:10-15

These verses are the origins of the church's teaching on being purified by fire after death. The image of fire seems to come from apocalyptic literature, but Paul takes it a step further, suggesting that every person will go through some kind of purification before meeting the Lord. We will know for sure when that day comes.

Read 1 Corinthians 3:16-23

Paul beautifully expresses how each person in the community is a temple, a dwelling place of God's Spirit. This indwelling of God is a precious gift. It calls for new behavior. Every Christian must revere the gift of God's life in them. Paul then concludes his reflections on wisdom.

Read 1 Corinthians 4:1-5

In this chapter, Paul defines his concept of a Christian leader and calls the Corinthian community to accept the leadership that he provides. He says a leader must be a servant, one who takes responsibility for faithfully "administrating" the mysteries of God. Since Paul has had to deal with the destructiveness of false leaders, as we saw in Galatians, he is very aware of the need for Christian leaders to be faithful to the truth. He went to Jerusalem to make sure that his teaching was one with the larger Christian church.

What are some criteria that help you discern true Christian leaders?

____

____

Read 1 Corinthians 4:6-21

Here Paul begins sharing his heart with the Corinthians. He has recently been through Galatia, where he was persecuted, slandered, and accused of being a false apostle. He does not want the same thing to happen among the Corinthian community. In simple imagery, he expresses his deep love for his people, reminding them that he gave them life in Christ. Paul refers to himself as their "father," not to take anything away from God the Father, but to express his love for them and to win their trust in his guidance and leadership. It is for this reason that Christians began calling their leaders "father." Only if we feel Paul's deep care and love will we understand this image.

What are some ways that you can affirm the people who give you life in Christ?

____

____

Read 1 Corinthians 5:1-8

In this section, Paul deals with the difficult issue of public sin within the Christian community. In his letter to the Galatians (6:1-10), Paul tells the community to "gently set the sinner right." In this case, his words are stronger and more radical, but his intent is the same. Paul's instruction in verse five is not intended to destroy the sinner. He believes that if the person is cast out of the community for a time, the urges of his flesh would be destroyed. He would then return to the community and thus save his spirit. With this understanding, we realize that Paul is doing what he feels is the best thing for this man in terms of his ultimate salvation. Out of concern for the life of the public sinner, as well as his concern for the life of the community (verses 6-8), Paul calls for a temporary separation. He wants all to be saved. The early church used this same pattern to lead public sinners to reconciliation with Christ.

In dealing with public serious sin, what means are appropriate for calling people to live by Christian values while at the same time ministering the forgiveness of Christ to them?

____

____

Read 1 Corinthians 5:9-13

Paul is aware that Christians cannot avoid associating with people whose values differ from their own. Christians may not judge by their standards those who do not know the teachings and values of Jesus. That, according to Paul, is God's job. Those who commit themselves to the Christian community, however, are responsible for living a life worthy of the name they bear. Although God is still the ultimate judge of each person's heart, Paul urges community members to call one another to a lifestyle that manifests the message of Jesus.

How do you apply this word to your daily life?

____

____

Read 1 Corinthians 6:1-11

As we have seen in Galatians 6:1-10, the early communities took on the responsibility of helping each other live according to Jesus' law of love. Paul explains here that people who have not been "consecrated and justified in the name of Jesus" cannot judge what is fitting behavior for a Christian. With gentleness and love, the Christian community was to bring one another before the Lord, whose words and teachings would lead them to judge themselves and be reconciled.

Read 1 Corinthians 6:12-20

Paul points out to the Corinthian community that uniting one's body with a prostitute is seriously wrong, since the body of a Christian is one with Christ. As members of Christ, the people in the community could no longer do the things that were acceptable, and probably even prevalent, among the other Corinthians. Christian moral conduct begins with an awareness that our bodies are one with Christ and a temple of his Spirit.

What do these verses say about sexual intimacy outside of marriage?

____

____

In Chapter 7, Paul expresses his understanding of Jesus' teaching on marriage and divorce. From verses 26, 29, 30, and 31, we come to understand that some of Paul's thoughts may be influenced by his belief that the second coming is not far off. His teachings are in agreement with Jesus' instruction on marriage and divorce (see Mark 10:2-12). As the church grew, there are indications that pastoral concessions were made concerning this teaching. The church would continually attempt to apply Jesus' message to the complex circumstances surrounding marital relationships.

Read 1 Corinthians 7:1-9
From these verses, we cannot tell if Paul was celibate or widowed. He does indicate that the ability to remain single is a gift from God. Perhaps his most revolutionary message in these verses is that husband and wife are equally obligated to each other. Christian husbands could no longer treat their wives as someone they owned, since both were equal before the Lord. This would place new responsibilities on both of them.

How would you define equality in a marital relationship?

____

____

Read 1 Corinthians 7:10-16
Paul quotes Jesus' teaching on marriage and divorce, but points out that this applies only to Christian marriages. Through the power of God's Spirit, Christians can live up to Jesus' teaching. As an apostle and teacher, Paul must apply Jesus' teaching to the situation he was bound to meet; namely,

the marriage between a Christian and non-Christian. In verse 14 he uses a principle from his Jewish background to explain that through the intimacy of the union, the believing spouse makes the children holy, thus making the unbelieving spouse holy. He clearly expresses his belief that God's main concern is for Christians to live peacefully. Throughout history the Christian church has attempted to apply this teaching to specific situations.

How would you apply this message to the situation of divorce and remarriage today?

____

____

Read 1 Corinthians 7:17-24
As we read Paul, we become aware of his conviction that being committed to Christ involves an inner transformation, a change of attitudes and values. In these verses, Paul points out that one's occupation need not change. He tells the Corinthians to serve the Lord wherever they find themselves.

Read 1 Corinthians 7:25-40
Here Paul expresses his opinion about virginity. He seems to have a negative view on marriage, seeing it as a consolation. However, this may be related to his belief that the second coming was imminent. More than anything, he wanted his people to be totally dedicated to the Lord. His advice to fathers who wondered about giving their daughters in marriage (verses 36-38) is very simple and caring.

Read 1 Corinthians 8:1-13
In this chapter, Paul advises the Corinthians concerning eating meat that has been offered to idols. It is interesting to note the way he disclaims the power of idols and turns his attention to the question of scandalizing others. Paul is very much aware of the importance and the power of Christian witness. Any action that may detract someone from the Lord, or cause a person to sin, is wrong in his eyes.

To what situations in your life might you apply this teaching?

____

____

Read 1 Corinthians 9:1-27
Up to this point in this letter, Paul has been teaching his people. In these verses he lets his feelings show. As in Galatia, someone has accused him of being a false apostle, and that touches a tender spot in the heart of a man who has given himself totally to the spreading of God's word. Paul's hurt is evident as he powerfully writes of his calling in Christ and all that he has surrendered so that others may be saved. His unselfish life witness and his strength of character speak loudly of the power of the Lord. Despite ridicule and persecution, he kept his eyes on the finish line.

Which of Paul's traits do you most seek to imitate?

____

____

Read 1 Corinthians 10:1-13
Again focusing his attention on his people, Paul encourages them not to give in to temptations. He assures them that with God's strength they can overcome any test.

Read 1 Corinthians 10:14-11:1
Because Paul loves his people, he does not want them to take part in worshiping idols. His desire is that they come to appreciate the cup and the bread of eucharist. The unity with Christ and with one another expressed in sharing the body and blood of Christ is central to the life of the Christian community. That sharing in Christ, he says, should discourage Christians from eating food offered to idols. Again, as in chapter eight, the emphasis is on giving good example.

What does sharing in eucharist mean for you?

____

____

Read 1 Corinthians 11:2-16
Paul uses categories from his Jewish background to explain the custom of women wearing headdresses during prayer, a seemingly insignificant issue. This custom seems to be related to the fact that women wore their hair longer, which, according to Paul, seemed to be more in keeping with nature. His description of the relationship between women and men in this section is rather confusing and quite unresolved. To pull any of these verses out of this context would only leave a person confused about Paul and about a simple custom of the early church.

The remaining verses of Chapter 11 deal with the central act of worship in the community: the celebration of the Lord's supper. Paul shares with his people what he received from the Lord concerning this meal.

Read 1 Corinthians 11:17-22
We get the impression from these verses that the Corinthian community was very human, tempted by selfishness even while celebrating eucharist. Their eating of the Lord's supper, which was to demonstrate unity and common sharing, was torn by divisions and self-indulgence. Paul firmly yet gently tells them that such behavior must change.

In what ways do you see the celebration of eucharist being less than a meal of unity and common sharing today?

____

____

Read 1 Corinthians 11:23-34
Paul indicates to his people that the words he is writing to them concerning eucharist come directly from the Lord. Jesus

had given his disciples the command to eat this meal in remembrance of his saving actions. It was central to the ongoing life and growth of the Christian community. Paul believed that if the members of the community did not assemble themselves prayerfully around their Lord and share in his body and blood, they would die. Paul was keenly aware that his real life and the life of the community came from the Lord. Since he loved his people so dearly, he wanted them to understand clearly the life-giving power of this meal. The growing church had to continually rediscover the truth of his words.

How central is the celebration of eucharist in your life? In your community?

____

____

Read 1 Corinthians 12:1-11
Within the Corinthian community as well as among other early Christian communities, people found themselves with new power and new abilities after experiencing the risen Lord. Paul knew that power well since it had transformed his life. He calls this power the Holy Spirit and describes the various ways that he has seen it manifested in the lives of Christian people. As people surrender their abilities to the Lord, the Spirit transforms them into gifts for the common good of all. While the gifts are many, even more than mentioned here, they all flow from the one and same Spirit of God.

How has the transforming power of the Spirit enabled you to minister to others?

____

____

Read 1 Corinthians 12:12-26
Paul uses the image of the human body to illustrate the beauty of diverse parts dependent on each other to form one entity. His vision for the members of the Corinthian community is that with their individual uniqueness they will form one body in Christ. They need each other's gifts to become a complete entity for the Lord. As we have seen earlier (Galatians 2:1-10), Paul also recognized the importance of unity among all the various Christian communities.

How do you see this image of the body acted out in your community? What is your part?

Read 1 Corinthians 12:27-31
There are various gifts manifested among community members, and there are also various occupations to which God calls his individual members. Every person must follow God's calling and use the gifts God has given him. The Corinthians sought after spiritual gifts and seemed to think that some gifts were greater than others. Paul alludes to this in verse 31a, where he writes: "You are striving after the greatest gifts." That was the source of their quarrel and divisions. Paul shows them a "better way." Paul teaches them to respect one another's gifts as equal, for only when each one's unique God-given gifts are manifested for the common good, will the community be a complete hymn of praise to their Lord.

Read 1 Corinthians 13:1-13
In simple, poetic style, Paul reflects on the beauty and steadfastness of true love. He had mentioned it earlier as one of the fruits of the Spirit (Galatians 5:22), and now he tells the Corinthians that it must be the underlying attitude with which they use their gifts. Paul had come to know the joys and pains of true love. He is aware that its value is eternal.

How often do you use the word "love" to mean something less than what Paul describes in this chapter?

____

____

Read 1 Corinthians 14:1-12
Because the Corinthians were striving for spiritual gifts, Paul tries to give them some instruction about when it is best to manifest them. He does not want to squelch anyone's gift. He gently tries to show the Corinthians that when they are gathered for worship, prophecy is more beneficial to the assembly than words uttered in tongues.

Read 1 Corinthians 14:13-25
Paul witnesses to the fact that he had experienced the beauty of the gift of tongues as a gift of praise to God. It is a way of allowing one's spirit to pray freely. He again points out that when gathered as a community, prophecy has a greater value than speaking in tongues because it proclaims God's word in an understandable way to those present.

Read 1 Corinthians 14:26-40
Here Paul gives some very practical instructions to the Corinthians concerning how they should conduct their prayer gatherings. Paul stresses that things be done in an orderly manner. He wants the people to benefit from their communal prayer. Apparently, some gatherings had become disorderly, with no one being instructed or encouraged. Verse 36 seems to indicate that on some occasions, women in the Corinthian community dominated the assembly. The customs of the communities of Palestine prohibited women from speaking publicly in their assemblies. With an eye toward maintaining unity and order, Paul tells the Corinthians to follow the custom of the larger church in this matter. His ultimate goal is that all be enriched and instructed in the Lord.

Do you feel that your church has a healthy balance between allowing people to manifest their gifts of prayer while also keeping order? Explain.

____

____

Chapter 15 deals with issues concerning the resurrection of Jesus and of all believers. Like the Thessalonians, the people of Corinth had questions about the resurrection. Some did not believe in the resurrection of Jesus, while others were concerned more about their own resurrection. To address these issues, Paul begins with the core teachings which had been handed down to him.

Read 1 Corinthians 15:1-4
In a few concise verses, Paul captures for the members of the community the fundamental truths of their faith life, namely, that Christ died for their sins, was buried, and rose again. By holding to these gospel truths, Paul assures the Corinthians that they will arrive at final salvation. Paul has just proclaimed the basic saving message of Jesus Christ. Feel the power of these words.

Read 1 Corinthians 15:5-11
To convince his readers of the reality of Jesus' resurrection, Paul mentions all of the people who saw his risen presence. More convincing than all of those people, however, was the fact that Paul himself saw the risen Lord. He did not doubt that Jesus rose from the dead. His life witness was clear evidence that Jesus was alive. Though he was born later than most of the other apostles and had persecuted the church, God favored him with a vision of his risen son. Paul's life and works would continue to proclaim that his favor was not fruitless.

In what ways has God favored you with evidence of his living presence?

____

____

Read 1 Corinthians 15:12-28

Having testified to the resurrection of Jesus, Paul assures the Corinthians that all who belong to Christ, who have faith in him, will be raised up with him. Christ's resurrection makes eternal life a hope and a reality for all who are one with him. Sin, upon entering the world, caused spiritual death and anxiety about physical death. Christ conquered sin and the effects of sin so that all who believe in him could feel the freedom of forgiveness and have the peace of knowing that they can live forever. There is eternal power in this message.

How have you seen this message bring peace to others or to yourself?

____

____

Read 1 Corinthians 15:29-34

It seems evident from verse 29 that the early communities baptized people with the name of someone who had died. Paul simply points out that this practice was based on a belief in the resurrection. We get the impression that from earliest times in the church, people believed in the communion of saints. Death was, for them, a passing to union with the Lord and all who lived with him. With a bit more personal feeling, Paul points out that he could not face the danger of death with such confidence if he did not believe in eternal life. Then he cautions the Corinthians about those who lead them away from the saving message of resurrection in Christ.

Read 1 Corinthians 15:35-49

The last question that Paul addresses concerning the resurrection is, "What is the form of one's resurrected body?" In verses five through seven of this chapter, he implied that Jesus' resurrected form was recognizable to those who knew him before his death. Paul now uses an image to speak of a reality that is beyond human terms. He explains that our resurrected body must be analogous to the new plant that springs forth from a seed that has died in the ground. While searching for words to express the inexpressible, Paul assures the Corinthians that their resurrected form will be glorious and incorruptible.

Read 1 Corinthians 15:50-58
Having courageously dealt with the mystery of death and resurrection, Paul now poetically summarizes his message. For those who believe in the resurrection, death had been conquered. The victory is Christ's. This conviction would make the Corinthians and all Christians unbelievably powerful in the face of persecution; it is impossible to kill a person who believes in eternal life.

How does the message of resurrection affect the way you live?

____

____

Read 1 Corinthians 16:1-24
Paul concludes this lengthy letter with some brief directives and some warm expressions of care. Mindful of the poor in the Jerusalem community, Paul reminds the members of the community to put aside whatever they can afford (see also Galatians 2:10). He then shares his future traveling plans with them, indicating his need to be renewed in their company. After urging the community to treat his associates well, he shares some greetings, and ends with an expression of his deep affection for his people. They were very special to him.

Paul has done some very practical and difficult teaching in this letter, while also sharing his own beliefs and convictions. His words continue to help people deal with the issues and challenges of living the Christian life. God continues to speak through him.

Summary Question

What teaching has spoken to you most powerfully through this letter?

____

____

Questions for Reflection and Discussion

1. What teaching has spoken to you most powerfully through this letter?

2. What do you see as significant issues within Christian communities today?

3. Can you recall an incident in which you expressed gentle love at a time when anger may have been expected?

4. How might you apply 1 Corinthians 1:10-13 to Christian communities today?

5. In what ways can you identify with the Corinthians?

6. What do the two images of 1 Corinthians 3:1-9 say to you?

7. What are some criteria that help you discern true Christian leaders?

8. What are some ways that you can affirm the people who give you life in Christ?

9. In dealing with public serious sin, what means are appropriate for calling people to live by Christian values while at the same time ministering the forgiveness of Christ to them?

10. How do you apply 1 Corinthians 5:9-13 to your daily life?

11. What does 1 Corinthians 6:12-20 say about sexual intimacy outside of marriage?

12. How would you define equality in a marital relationship?

13. How would you apply 1 Corinthians 7:10-16 to the situation of divorce and remarriage today?

14. To what situations in your life might you apply the teaching in 1 Corinthians 8:1-13?

15. Which of Paul's traits do you most seek to imitate?

16. What does sharing in eucharist mean for you?

17. In what ways do you see the celebration of the eucharist today as less than a meal of unity and common sharing?

18. How central is the celebration of eucharist in your life? In your community?

19. How has the transforming power of the Spirit enabled you to minister to others?

20. How do you see Paul's image of the body acted out in your community? What is your part?

21. How often do you use the word "love" to mean something less than what Paul describes in 1 Corinthians 13:1-13?

22. Do you feel that your church has a healthy balance between allowing people to manifest their gifts of prayer while also keeping order? Explain.

23. In what ways has God favored you with evidence of his living presence?

24. How have you seen 1 Corinthians 15:12-28 bring peace to others or to yourself?

25. How does the message of resurrection affect the way you live?

Chapter 6

The Second Letter to the Corinthians

All loving and caring Father, you constantly anoint us with your mercy and strengthen us in your love. May your message of comfort and consolation touch our hearts as we reflect on the words of this letter. As you assured Paul of your caring presence in his suffering and times of weakness, so may we be encouraged and strengthened in our times of difficulty and pain. May we treasure the presence of Christ your son in our hearts until we arrive at final union with you forever and ever. Amen.

Paul probably wrote this letter not too long after writing 1 Corinthians (c. A.D. 57). As mentioned in the introduction to that letter, it may well be the fourth letter he wrote to them. From 2 Corinthians 7:5 and 9:2-4, it seems evident that Paul wrote this letter from Macedonia, a region in northern Greece. Since writing 1 Corinthians, Paul had apparently heard more unsettling news about the Corinthians and received some criticism regarding his style and authority. In addition to that, he has experienced more persecution in Asia. Because of these incidents, Paul expresses much more feeling in this letter than in 1 Corinthians. As such, 2 Corinthians is more like his letters to the Galatians and Philippians. We experience his hurt; we hear his anger; we feel his sincere love.

In this letter, Paul speaks much about his sufferings. His words reveal the pains in his heart, but his acceptance of those pains reveals the power of his unity with Christ. This letter, more than any other, portrays the inner strength of Paul, a strength that could only come from Christ himself. To those who suffer, it brings a message of comfort and a vision of eternal life.

Read 2 Corinthians 1:1-11
Following his usual greeting, Paul begins immediately to speak about his recent trouble in Asia, the suffering it caused, and the way it led him to a deeper trust in God. Paul has a way of saying a great deal in a few lines. In the midst of speaking about his sufferings, he articulates a simple yet profound understanding of redemptive suffering (verses 5-7). This understanding is evident throughout his letters. He truly believed that because Christians are one in Christ, their acceptance of suffering to spread the gospel could be a source of encouragement and consolation for others. His words left the church with a vision for putting meaning into the hard realities of Christian living. Not only did Paul see that others could benefit from his acceptance of suffering, but he was also aware that through his suffering he had come to trust more totally in the real source of all life. These verses give us an inside picture of what made Paul so strong.

What occasions of suffering have you made redemptive for others, or beneficial for your own growth in the Lord?

____

____

Read 2 Corinthians 1:12-24
These verses give us the context in which Paul writes 2 Corinthians. Apparently, Paul said that he was going to visit the Corinthian community and then decided not to do so. Some of the members of the community seem to have been upset with that decision, even to the point of accusing Paul of being insincere and selfish (1:17). We can imagine his deep hurt at these com-

ments, since he would have done anything to benefit his people. Verses 21-24 give us an indication that Paul avoided visiting them for their own good, so they might depend more totally on God rather than on him. He did not want to dominate them, but to allow them to grow freely in an ever deeper faith. Paul knew well how to lead people in Christian growth, always turning their attention to the real author of life, not to himself. With gentleness, he affirms the growing faith of his people and reminds them of his great love for them.

What do these verses say to you about Christian leadership?

____

____

Read 2 Corinthians 2:1-4
Although Paul did not visit the Corinthians, it seems that he did write them a letter. That "tearful" letter, as mentioned earlier, was apparently not preserved for us in its original form. Some scholars believe that Chapters 10-13 of 2 Corinthians are part of that letter. In any case, the purpose of that letter, as Paul puts it, was "to help you realize the great love I bear you." In a certain sense, that expresses the purpose of all Paul's letters. They are love letters to his "children." In them, Paul expresses his love and God's love for his people; he encourages and affirms them and us.

Read 2 Corinthians 2:5-11
In these verses, Paul expands upon his understanding of reconciliation, which he briefly mentioned in 1 Corinthians 5:1-8. The sinful person had to be dealt with, but once he repented, it was the community's obligation to welcome him back and reaffirm their love for him. The ultimate purpose was to bring one another to final salvation in Christ. The early church used this model to minister the mercy of Jesus.

Read 2 Corinthians 2:12-17
Paul powerfully expresses his awareness that God directed his whole life. Again using an image, he proclaims the life-giving

effects of those who speak and live in Christ. Their witness is a refreshing fragrance to those on the road to salvation.

What people in your life have been a refreshing fragrance to you?

____

____

Read 2 Corinthians 3:1-3
Some people questioned Paul's authority, accusing him of not having any letter of recommendation from anyone. Paul turns the accusation into words of affirmation by telling the community that they are his letter of recommendation, "written not with ink but by the Spirit of the living God, not on tablets of stone but on tablets of flesh in the heart." What a powerful message! Their life witness in Christ was the clearest evidence that Paul was authentic. His letter of recommendation would speak forever.

Who are your letters of recommendation?

____

____

Read 2 Corinthians 3:4-18
In these verses, Paul summarizes his teaching about salvation, a theme he wrote about to the Galatians and would expand in his letter to the Romans. According to Paul, the written law of Moses would ultimately lead to spiritual death because it did not contain the necessary grace to carry out the regulations it prescribed. The old law was a written word; the new law was a love relationship. God graciously initiated this new covenant relationship in Christ, a relationship that manifested God's glory and expressed his desire to be one with his people. Those who accept Christ as God's son, who unveil their eyes, are em-

powered through his Spirit to carry out his new "law of love." Through the Spirit, Christians would be given the power to be transformed into the image of Christ himself. That power dwells among us today.

Read 2 Corinthians 4:1-7
Perhaps one of the richest images of a Christian is expressed here in the picture of an earthen vessel containing the treasure of Christ. Paul beautifully portrays the preciousness of the presence of Christ and he indicates the fragility of those who "contain" him. Aware of the treasure he possesses, Paul does not give in to discouragement or underhanded practices. With faithful perseverance, he continues to draw on the strength of the Lord. His image and his life continue to speak to us.

What does Paul's image say to you?

____

____

Read 2 Corinthians 4:8-18
In poetic style, Paul speaks of his sufferings, which he endures with the strength of the Lord. As we have seen, he and his disciples faced great opposition, but with the Lord's help, it never destroyed them. Paul taught people to face all situations with confidence and trust, knowing that the same power that raised Jesus from the dead was in them. With their eyes fixed on Christ, they could face all things. To those who suffer, this word brings refreshment and comfort.

Read 2 Corinthians 5:1-10
Paul uses the image of a tent to express his vision of real life. He is completely confident that there is eternal life in the Lord. His words give us evidence that he longed to be in that "heavenly habitation," yet his life expressed the power of knowing it was there. These verses continue to be a source of strength and consolation for those facing the pains of separation brought on by death. The promise of a heavenly dwelling with the Lord gives undying power to Christian life.

Has this message ever brought comfort to you or someone you know? If so, explain.

____

____

Read 2 Corinthians 5:11-21

Here Paul powerfully reflects on the meaning of the death and resurrection of Jesus. Christians knew that historically Jesus had been crucified, but it was primarily through Paul's reflections that they came to realize what that death meant for them. Through the reflections of people like Paul, the early Christians came to understand that they were new creations, freed from their former bondage to sin by the death and resurrection of Jesus. Paul's faith vision of God's plan of reconciliation brought many others to believe in the saving effects of Christ's dying and rising. In simple fashion, Paul then tells his people that each of them has been given the "ministry of reconciliation." Endowed with a great gift, they are called to be a giving people. As ambassadors for Christ, they are called to forgive and reconcile others as he did. "Regular people" were chosen to be ambassadors for the one who had set them free.

In your life, where do you feel called to minister reconciliation?

____

____

Read 2 Corinthians 6:1-13

Paul speaks frankly with the Corinthians expressing a bit of his hurt at the coldness he has felt from some of them. In opening his heart to them, we get a picture of what he went through to minister God's word. We see the irony of those who discredited him. His honesty and sincerity are evident in his words. With patience and deep love, he makes the first move toward a renewed friendship with his people. He is truly a minister of reconciliation.

Read 2 Corinthians 6:14-7:1

This section seems to be out of context, and some scholars believe that it may be an excerpt from one of Paul's lost letters. It addresses the issue of Christians dealing with non-Christians. While Paul was aware that contact with unbelievers was bound to happen (1 Corinthians 5:10), he tells the Corinthians not to engage intimately in their way of life. Using Old Testament references to Jewish ritual purity, Paul expresses his desire to have the Corinthians remain free of moral corruption. He encourages his people to fellowship with other believers, but he is also aware that a true loving witness could lead another person to salvation (1 Corinthians 7:16).

Read 2 Corinthians 7:2-16

These verses give us a clearer picture of the context in which 2 Corinthians was written, and they show us the beautiful sensitivity of Paul. In verse eight, Paul mentions the letter he wrote in sorrow and anguish (see 2 Corinthians 2:4), which apparently caused the community some grief for a time. Paul has a unique way of emphasizing the good that comes from necessary pain in the Lord (verses 8-9). We get the impression that his letter brought the Corinthians to repentance, which was for their ultimate good. Apparently, Paul sent Titus to deliver the letter and to deal with a situation that needed correcting. Paul is elated to hear that the situation is resolved, but he is even more joyful that the community had come to accept Titus, his disciple. Paul was already training someone to take his place. It must have warmed his heart to hear Titus speak of the Corinthians with such affection. Paul knew then that Titus would make a powerful minister of God.

What message comes to you from this section?

____

____

Read 2 Corinthians 8:1-15
Paul addresses the issue of the collection for the poor in Jerusalem (1 Corinthians 16:1-4) and encourages the members of the community to be as generous as they can. His request for generosity is based on the generosity of Jesus, who "made himself poor though he was rich, so that you might become rich by his poverty." Paul is deeply aware of the abundant gifts of God and is also in touch with the needs of the poor within the universal church (see Galatians 2:10). He expresses to the Corinthians his vision of the larger church and asks them to share in the needs of all their brothers and sisters in Christ. According to their means, they were to give to the poor, that there might be equality.

How do you apply Paul's vision and request to your own situation?

____

____

Read 2 Corinthians 8:16-24
Those who administered funds from such a collection had to be trustworthy, and Paul recommends Titus and the brother with him. Confidently, Paul assures the Corinthians that Titus and his helper are honest men.

Read 2 Corinthians 9:1-15
In this chapter, Paul somewhat repeats himself as he continues to exhort the Corinthians to be generous. Paul is boasting to the people of northern Greece, Macedonia, telling them that the Corinthians who live in the southern region of Achaia will make a bountiful gift to the poor. He then uses the image of sowing seeds to imply that their generosity will be rewarded. As a final note, Paul mentions that their gift will bring others to praise God. We get the impression from Romans 15:25-27 that the collection was a success.

In addition to giving money to the poor, what other successes do you think Paul saw in this collection?

Read 2 Corinthians 10:1-11:6
Did you notice Paul's change of tone as you began reading this chapter? Does it sound as if we are reading a different letter, or has Paul just decided to address another issue? As mentioned earlier, some scholars believe that chapters 10-13 could be part of an earlier letter, perhaps even the one referred to in 2:4 and 7:8. Only God, and Paul, know for sure. Whatever the context, these chapters show us the same side of Paul we saw in his letter to the Galatians. His feelings will become more and more evident as we read through this section.

Read 2 Corinthians 10:1-18
As we read these verses, we can understand why Paul is hurt and even angry. Some people have come among the community at Corinth and started undermining his authority as they had done in Galatia. False teachers could easily disturb these new communities, and they did. Apparently, they accused Paul of "weak human behavior," stating that although his letters were forceful, in person he was unimpressive. It seems that they were unimpressed with his gentle love. In verses 1-11, Paul explains his reason for acting as he did, but after that, his sarcasm begins to show. He is not impressed with people who have a need to recommend themselves and boast of work they have not done. Paul makes these observations with the assurance of a man who knows the Lord. He has no doubt that Jesus has sent him and recommended him to care for these people. It is this recommendation that gives him strength. He will do all in his power, with the power of the Lord, to safeguard the growing faith of the Corinthians.

How do you think the Lord "recommends" people for Christian leadership today?

____

____

Read 2 Corinthians 11:1-3

Paul knows that boasting is "foolish" but he does it to benefit the community. He will do anything for them. His concern is for their ultimate happiness. In beautiful imagery, he describes how he, as father, wedded his community to Christ. As a good father of his time, Paul encourages his community to continue in "sincere and complete devotion to Christ." He has taken the Old Testament image describing the love relationship between God and the Jewish people and applied it to Christ and his people. The image evokes the call to faithful love.

Read 2 Corinthians 11:4-15

From these verses, we get the impression that Paul feels somewhat betrayed by the people he loves. Though he would never abandon them, he gives them some strong words of reprimand. He is angry with the false apostles who came among them, but he is also disappointed that the community accepted them so easily. In polished sarcasm, he makes his feelings known. Paul uses sharp words, but he does so to rescue his people from false teaching. The Corinthians could not help but get his message, just as they could not help but feel his deep love. It is evident that no false apostles would stop him from loving his people and doing his work in the way in which he felt called. His persistence and faithful love are evident.

How do you go about reprimanding those you love?

____

____

Read 2 Corinthians 11:16-33

The words and activities of the false apostles certainly touched some sensitive areas in Paul. He must have felt close to the Corinthians to share his feelings so openly. Using a manner of boasting that he says even the Lord does not desire, Paul goes about expressing what lies deep within his heart. Generally, he does not boast, but when he does, he boasts of his sufferings, not of his achievements as others do. If anyone had given himself in suffering and persecution to spread Christ's message, Paul had done it. He endured it all to benefit others. That is redemptive suffering. We can feel the investment he makes in his people. They are his life, and his love for them is his strength. His "foolish talk" in these verses is evidence that he is a true minister of Christ.

Read 2 Corinthians 12:1-7a

Paul is apparently referring here to some mystical experience that he had some time ago. He describes the event in a unique style, referring to himself in the third person. It seems evident that the experience mentioned here is different from Paul's conversion, which began his life in the Lord.

Read 2 Corinthians 12:7b-10

These verses express the conviction that made Paul strong. He had come to realize that when he admitted his weakness, Christ's power reached its perfection in him. This realization not only gave him strength, it would also be the strength and power of all Christians. It is truly a message that gives life.

We can take a moment to conjecture what exactly the "thorn in the flesh" was, but after centuries of study and reflection, even the scholars do not know for sure. What seems more significant is that once Paul realized that it was there to stay, he used it to keep himself humble before his God. Somehow, he was able to find a good purpose for any situation in life. That ability brought him contentment, a contentment he proclaims for all who trust the creator.

In what situations of weakness have you experienced the power of Christ?

Read 2 Corinthians 12:11-18
Paul draws his firey speech to a close with a few pointed questions and a powerful expression of his love. He reminds the Corinthians that he did perform the works of an apostle among them, never taking advantage of them in any way. With a bit of poignancy, he questions whether he has loved them "too much," and yet each of them knew that it was his love that had changed their lives. As a father, he had taught them to love Father-God. He would gladly "spend himself and be spent" that all might come to know the life that was theirs in Christ. What a powerful description of Christian ministry!

In what ways do you feel called to spend yourself for the life of others?

Read 2 Corinthians 12:19-13:10
Paul makes it clear that all his "foolish talk" and sharp words were meant not to destroy them, but to bring them back on the road to Christ. He wants them to put their lives in order not only because he was coming to visit them, but because as Christians they were to live in accordance with the teachings of Christ. Those who had fallen into old practices were called to examine themselves and repent of their ways. Paul wants them to be "built up to completion" that they might know the peace of being one with the Lord.

Read 2 Corinthians 13:11-13
Paul ends his letter with some brief directives and a blessing.

Having shared his deep feelings, he now wishes the Corinthians well and tells them to encourage each other. His final words of blessing are the richest of any in his letters. He wishes the Corinthians the grace of Jesus, the love of the Father, and the fellowship of the Holy Spirit – all that they need to arrive at final salvation. Implied in this blessing is also an indication that by this time the church was beginning to speak of the Holy Spirit as a distinct person from the father and Jesus, yet one with them. From early on, Christians experienced the triune presence of God, and they would gradually become comfortable describing what they experienced.

2 Corinthians makes us aware that Paul was human, yet we realize that in his very humanness God used him as a powerful instrument of his word. Paul's sharp sarcasm and foolish boasting may not have been the methods of Jesus, but his acceptance of suffering and his generous spending of himself for others tell us that he loved with the love of God. He would visit the Corinthian community once more, and when he did, they would know that a true minister of Christ was in their midst.

Summary Questions

What does this letter say to you about Christian ministry?

____

____

For you, what is the strongest message in this letter?

____

____

Questions for Discussion and Reflection

1. What does this letter say to you about Christian ministry?

2. For you, what is the strongest message in this letter?

3. What occasions of suffering have you made redemptive for others, or beneficial for your own growth in the Lord?

4. What does 2 Corinthians 1:12-24 say to you about Christian leadership?

5. What people in your life have been a refreshing fragrance to you?

6. What people are your "letters of recommendation"?

7. What does Paul's image in 2 Corinthians 4:1-7 say to you?

8. Has the message of 2 Corinthians 5:1-10 ever brought comfort to you or someone you know? If so, explain.

9. In your life, where do you feel called to minister reconciliation?

10. What message comes to you from 2 Corinthians 7:2-16?

11. How do you apply Paul's vision and request in 2 Corinthians 8:1-15 to your own situation?

12. In addition to giving money to the poor, what other successes do you think Paul saw in the collection mentioned in 2 Corinthians 9:1-15?

13. How do you think the Lord "recommends" people for Christian leadership today?

14. How do you go about reprimanding those you love?

15. In what situations of weakness have you experienced the power of Christ?

16. In what ways do you feel called to spend yourself for the life of others?

Chapter 7

THE LETTER TO THE ROMANS

Father, you blessed us with the gift of your son that we might be set free from sin and enjoy the peace of life with you. Open our hearts and minds to the power and beauty of that gift as we contemplate your word. Renew our faith in your saving love. Fill each of us with an abundance of your grace so that nothing may ever separate us from you. With the help of your Spirit, may we come to arrive at final salvation in you forever and ever. Amen.

After writing to the Corinthians, Paul visits them once more. During his stay with the Corinthian community (A.D. 58), he writes his Letter to the Romans. Paul had never been to Rome, but he planned to visit there on his way to Spain after taking the church collection to the poor Christians in Jerusalem (see Romans 15:18-26). Paul's plans were changed when he was arrested by the Jews in Jerusalem for bringing Gentiles into the temple. As a Roman citizen, he appealed to Caesar and eventually was taken to Rome for his trial.

Rome was the capital city of the known world and the center of trade. The Roman community was probably established by Christian traders and workers coming into Rome. Paul did not know the Roman community as well as he knew the other communities to which he had written. For that reason, this letter does not contain the personal feelings evident in some of the other letters. Paul writes it to introduce himself to the community and to give them his understanding of the basic gospel message. The main theme of this letter is the relationship between Judaism and Christianity, a theme that Paul addressed in writing to the Galatians. Both religions claimed to be the way of salvation. In orderly fashion, Paul presents his vision of Christianity as a way of salvation for all people. The letter to the Romans is more like a treatise than a letter. It does not deal with any specific problems in the Roman community, but rather gives general instructions concerning issues that Paul met in other places. Apparently, the entire letter was written at one time, except for the last chapter. All the names mentioned in the last chapter do not seem to fit in the Roman community. We will see more of this later.

Read Romans 1:1-7

In his opening verse, Paul describes himself to the Romans. His life has given evidence that he is truly a servant of Christ in caring for his people. He was called to be an apostle by Christ himself and was set apart before his birth to proclaim the "gospel of God." Paul then indicates that this gospel of salvation is part of a divine plan beginning in the Old Testament and brought to fulfillment in Jesus Christ through his resurrection. Having introduced himself and Christ, Paul blesses the members of the Roman community by assuring them that they have been called to holiness by God. If any of them had ever felt burdened about being "regular people," Paul had a way of setting them free with the knowledge that they were "beloved of God."

How would you introduce yourself to a Christian community?

____

____

Read Romans 1:8-15

Apparently, Paul has heard of the faith evident in the Roman community and he thanks God for their widespread witness.

He indicates his desire to come among them to give and receive spiritual benefit. He knows the power of Christian encouragement and admits that he needs it as much as others do.

What spiritual benefits do you experience from sharing a common faith with someone?

____

____

Read Romans 1:16-17

Paul is not ashamed of the gospel. He has experienced its power to change his life. To express his conviction that all who believe in Christ are justified or made right with God, he paraphrases Habakkuk 2:4. Through living the gospel message, believers are led by God to final salvation with him. Recall that in Paul's understanding, justification is the "already" and salvation is the "not yet." He had written about this issue in his letter to the Galatians (2:15-3:14), and now here addresses it more extensively (1:16-11:36). In orderly fashion, Paul presents his teaching on justification by faith in Christ. He begins by expressing his understanding of humanity without the redeeming power of Christ.

Read Romans 1:18-32

Paul is convinced that the pagans should have been able to arrive at faith in God, since his power and presence are evident in all creation. Even if they did not know his name, they should have glorified and thanked the creator. Paul believes that because they did not respond to their ability to know God, God "delivered them up in their lust to unclean practices." He sees such practices as these leading to death. In Paul's mind, every person has some chance to know God, and to the extent that he refuses that gift, he is responsible.

What are some ways that a non-believer might come to experience God in creation?

____

____

Read Romans 2:1-16

In this section, Paul points out that the Jews cannot make judgments against the pagans, for in doing so, they would be condemning themselves. In the final judgment, all will be dealt with according to their ability to know God's law and their response to that knowledge. In that way, God shows no favoritism. In verses 14-16, Paul indicates his belief that all people by "instinct" have some knowledge of what is good and right. Only God knows to what extent that is true and to what extent people have allowed that knowledge to guide their lives.

It might be easiest to understand Paul's point here if we read to the end of this section.

Read Romans 2:17-3:20

You might wonder why Paul speaks so often about the Jews in this letter. Recall that many Jews of this time were teaching that only through their law were people made right with God. They felt as if they were the only "chosen people." Paul tries to show both the Jews and the Gentiles in the community at Rome that, through faith in Jesus, all are made right with God. He attempts to broaden their vision of the saving mercy of God. According to his understanding, Jewish law only points out what actions are sinful (3:20). It has no power to help people act rightly. If the Jews who know the law disobey it, they dishonor God (2:17-24). If they are circumcised but do not follow God's command, it means nothing (2:25-29). Because the Jews have the word of God (3:1-2), Paul believes that they should have an advantage, but this is true only if that word leads them to faith in Jesus. He goes on to point out that God is just. No one has to sin to make his justice visible (3:5-8). Paul quotes a number of Old Testament references to confirm his conviction that before Christ all people were under the dominion of sin. The law only pointed out sin, while through Christ, Christians are set free of sin and reconciled with God.

Read Romans 3:21-31

Here Paul articulates his vision of God's gift of redemption or justification that is made possible through the death and resurrection of Jesus. It is a profound statement about the goodness of God and the purpose of Jesus' redemptive mission. God made it possible for Jews and Gentiles to be freed from sin through Christ. Jews could no longer boast about observing their law as if it made them righteous. Now, together with all people, they would be justified through their faith in Jesus Christ. The community at Rome, and indeed all Christians, could rejoice in the message that in Christ they had been offered the gift of eternal life with God. It was up to them to decide whether or not they would accept that gift.

How does this message of justification in Christ strengthen you on the road to salvation?

____

____

Read Romans 4:1-25

In this chapter, Paul uses the example of Abraham to substantiate his argument that faith in God leads to justification. The Jews thought that they were made right with God through their blood relationship with Abraham and their observance of Jewish law. As Paul had pointed out in his letter to the Galatians (3:6-18), Abraham was made right with God through his faith even before he knew any laws (4:10). Thus, he is the father of all who believe. Like Abraham, Christians are justified through their faith in the God who raised Jesus from the dead. This must have been a very powerful argument for Jews who held Abraham in highest esteem as their "father." Now all Christians could look to him as a model of faith and trust in God.

Read Romans 5:1-11

Having finished his teaching on justification, Paul goes on to speak about salvation. He assures the Romans that if Christ loved them enough to die for them while they were sinners, they should be confident that he will stay with them as they journey toward salvation. From experience, Paul tells them that with the strength of God's love "poured out in their hearts," they can endure all things. They have access, through Christ, to all the grace they will need for their Christian journey. Using that gift, they can arrive at eternal salvation.

In what ways do you feel the graced presence of Jesus strengthening you on your life journey?

____

____

Read Romans 5:12-21
This section might make more sense if we understand Paul's view of salvation history and the law. In Paul's view, there was sin in the world since the time of Adam. However, when Moses came and gave the law, the awareness of sin was increased because then people knew what they should do. The law made sin more visible; however, it did not take sin away. That happened through God's gracious gift of Jesus.

Read Romans 5:12-21 again
Paul contrasts Adam and Jesus to point out the tremendous gift of Jesus' redemption. The gift of redemption is greater than the offense. The accent is on the "much more" (5:15-17). God's gift of love is "much more" than any human offense. Through the obedience of Jesus to the father's will, all who believe are set free of sin and its effects, namely, spiritual death. Paul experienced this gift of redemption in his life and spoke of it with gratitude and conviction. These words make it clear for all Christians that the love of God expressed in Jesus has won the victory over sin.

Through what means do you experience the gift of God's reconciliation in your community?

____

____

Read Romans 6:1-11

In simple imagery, Paul explains how Christians, through their baptism, have shared in the death and resurrection of Jesus. He reflects on how baptism is like the burying of one's old self in order to receive the new life of resurrection, a life that will never die. Because Christians have expressed their death to sin in baptism, they must seek to live their new life patterned after Christ. In him, death has no more power over them (see 1 Corinthians 15:55). The church would often use Paul's words to express the richness and power of baptism.

Read Romans 6:12-23

Paul tells the Romans that their freedom from the law through baptism does not mean that they are free to sin. Even though they no longer have to follow the detailed laws and practices of Judaism, they do have to obey the law of God. They still must make personal efforts to avoid sin, but with the grace of Christ, those efforts would bring them to eternal life. From his life, Paul was aware that Christ supplied the power for him to change his old ways. That was God's gift. Every Christian had to use that gift to arrive at eternal life.

How do you use Christ's power to overcome sin in your life?

____

____

Read Romans 7:1-13

Paul's words, especially his words about the law, can best be understood in their historical context. He is speaking to "men who know the law," namely, Jews who knew the law of Moses. Recall that Paul understood this law as a signpost which, when it was given through Moses, only made sin more visible. It only told people what was wrong and in that way, Paul says it brought sin to life, which brought death to people. The law had no power to free people from sin. For Christians, that power comes from Christ, through his death on the cross and resurrection from the dead. The more we understand Paul's concepts, the more we will understand his deep appreciation for Christ.

It might be helpful to note that in all these chapters on sin and the law, Paul is not trying to give definitions; he is trying to describe his understanding of and experiences with these realities. He hopes his words will help the Romans deal with the same realities. His focus is on the new life they have in Christ, and he wants them to experience, as he has, the power flowing from his resurrection.

Read Romans 7:14-25

Here Paul describes his experience of sin and temptation. In a way, he is describing the experience of most, if not all, Christians. Because he finds himself doing things he does not want to do, Paul concludes that sin must reign within his being. In these verses, he captures the very human struggle of getting one's body to do what one's mind knows to be right. Have any of you ever felt that struggle? Paul is aware that within himself he does not have the power to root out sin, and thus in humble desperation he cries out to the one who gives him strength for all things: Jesus Christ. The Romans would have known from these verses that Paul was a real person struggling as they were to change their old ways. Paul's message gives them and us the hope that with the power of Christ, the "new person" will gradually emerge. This is the message of chapter eight.

What things can you do to gradually root out sin from your life?

____

____

Read Romans 8:1-13
What the old law could not supply, the "law of the spirit" could, namely, the vitality and power to live out what the law says is right. In that sense, the Spirit is not a law but rather the life-giving power of God. In fact, according to Paul, it is the same power that "raised Christ from the dead." While there are still tendencies of the flesh of temptations within the lives of Christians, they have been gifted with the power of God's Spirit to handle them. That Spirit will lead them toward real life and peace. What a beautiful gift!

Read Romans 8:14-17
Paul tells the Romans what he had told the Galatians (Galatians 4-6). As Christians led by the Spirit of God, they not only enjoy new freedom, they also share a new relationship with God himself. They can call him "daddy" (Abba), knowing that he loves and cares for them.

What are your feelings as you reflect on God as a warm, loving "daddy"?

____

____

Read Romans 8:18-27
Paul focuses on the glory of God that will be revealed at some time. He believes that all his sufferings are nothing compared with what it will be like to see and experience the final presence of God. The whole created world, according to Paul, eagerly awaits that day. The Spirit is the "first fruits" or the guarantee that final salvation will happen. Paul assures the Romans that through the power of the Spirit, they can patiently endure whatever is necessary to arrive at eternal life. He is aware that in times of weakness, the Spirit of God is very strong.

Read Romans 8:28-39
Here Paul eloquently expresses his deep faith and trust in God. He has a strong belief that God can make something good come out of every event. Those who live life with God's vi-

sion, as Paul did, are able to see and appreciate that goodness. Paul powerfully proclaims to the Romans and to all Christians that neither anyone nor anything could separate them from the love of God. There is life-giving strength in these words. In the assurance of God's love, all things can be overcome. Paul's life witness shows us that he is speaking from experience. Our experience of God's love tells us that his message is true.

Describe a bad experience in which you were able to see God bring about some good.

____

____

Paul devotes the next three chapters to explaining his understanding of the Jews' rejection of Jesus. It must have been a puzzling and significant issue to the early Christians. To us, who might not feel the significance of this issue, these chapters may seem quite tedious. They do, however, accent the desire of God to lead all people to salvation in him. His love is universal.

Read Romans 9:1-5

These few verses make it clear to the Romans that Paul is still a Jew at heart. Even though he had died to the Jewish law and was born anew in Christ, he still had a deep love for his ancestry. He was willing to give anything to have the Jews know the power of Christ's resurrection.

In what ways can you identify with Paul's feelings about his ancestry?

____

____

Read Romans 9:6-33

Paul knows his Jewish bible well, and he uses it extensively to express his case. According to his vision, God chose the Jews and gave them prophets so that they might be a model for leading all people to justification in Christ. God was not unfair in choosing the Jews. It was simply his method to bring all people to himself. The Jews, who should have had an advantage in recognizing and believing Jesus as Lord, became so caught up with the literal observance of the law, that many refused to accept him. Paul effectively uses the image of a stone in Jerusalem (Zion) to help visualize his point. The Jews, who should have been able to build on what they learned from their temple in Jerusalem, ended up "stumbling" over that very teaching. In "stumbling," however, they did not "fall forever" (Romans 11:11-12), but only faltered for a time in order that they might come back and build, not alone, but with the Gentiles. The Jews and Gentiles together would build the "new Jerusalem," the church, through their faith in Christ, the universal savior. What an eloquent picture! What an affirming image!

How do you participate in building the "new Jerusalem"?

____

____

Read Romans 10:1-13

The Jews had refused God's way of justification in Christ, but Paul is still hopeful that they will not be lost forever. Paul wittingly plays on the words of Moses in the Torah (Deuteronomy 30:11-14) to show that no one has to scale the heights or plunder the depths in order to be justified. Christ has already done that in his life, death, and resurrection. Paul then summarizes his earlier teaching that faith leads to justification, and in confessing that faith through a good life witness, one can hope to arrive at final salvation.

Read Romans 10:14-21

Paul knows that if people are to believe in Christ, they must hear the gospel message. His life and travels make that evident. He experienced the beauty of those who journey with "good news." Having heard the message, it was up to the individual to accept it. That was the step that the Jews refused to take.

In what ways have you ever experienced the frustration of not being able to "force" someone to believe?

____

____

Read Romans 11:1-10
In these verses, Paul uses an Old Testament event to support his belief that God will not totally reject the Jewish people. In God's saving of a remnant, he sees a sign that God would always be merciful, despite rejection. Paul believes that God does not give up on anyone. This brief example may speak to us as people constantly in need of God's forgiveness.

Read Romans 11:11-36
As mentioned earlier, Paul now completes his image of the stone on Zion (Romans 9:6-33). He then addresses the Gentiles of the Roman community and uses an image they could understand to indicate their position in the saving plan of God. In Paul's image, the Gentiles are like branches grafted onto the tree of God's saving plan. Paul uses this image to point out to the Gentiles that they are to respect their roots of salvation and be abundantly grateful to God for making them a part of his life. Paul wants no one to be conceited, but rather to recognize that all are in the same position without the generous redeeming mercy of God. In a beautiful hymn of praise (verses 33-36), Paul sums up this section on the saving plan of God. He is awed by the wisdom and magnificence of God's ways.

When do you take time to thank God for his awesome, saving mercy?

____

____

Having finished his treatise on justification (Romans 1:18-11:36), Paul now tells the Romans what that means for their everyday lives. While it was their faith in Christ that brought them justification, it will be their lifestyle that will bring them final salvation in him. Paul takes these next chapters to explain exactly what that lifestyle entails. His directives speak to all Christians.

Read Romans 12:1-21

Because of God's gift in Christ, the Christians of Rome are to be transformed. They are not to act like those who do not know the saving power of Jesus. Their new way of life as believers would be a constant hymn of worship to God. As Paul told the Corinthians (1 Corinthians 12), so he now tells the Romans that they should use all of their gifts in unity to build up all people in Christ. Whatever their gifts, they are to use them in love. Paul conveys to them all he has heard from the Lord and has come to appreciate as the way to real life. He expresses his love for the Romans by sharing with them what he believes is the way to genuine happiness.

Which directive speaks most to your heart?

____

____

Read Romans 13:1-7

Paul's words about government authority are very much like those of Jesus. Paul tells the community in Rome that they are to obey their civil leaders, paying taxes and showing respect as is required. His understanding of authority seems to stem from his idea of the divine right of kings. This was the Jewish belief that kings or rulers received their authority from God; therefore, as his representatives, kings had to be obeyed. The early Christians would have to wrestle with these words, especially when the Roman government required them, under pain of death, to worship the emperor. There are times that Paul's words would take second place to the commandments of God. Christians today still live with the pains of reconciling these two teachings.

In what situations do you feel that a Christian has the right or obligation to disobey his or her government?

____

____

Read Romans 13:8-14

In a very simple and brief way, Paul summarizes God's law of love. He then indicates his belief that Christ's second coming may not be far off. He wants all people to be "clothed" in the virtues of Christ on that day.

Read Romans 14:1-15:13

In these verses, Paul applies the law of love to the issue of eating "unclean" food. Paul's main concern is that Christians do not scandalize or make judgments regarding this issue (see also 1 Corinthians 8:1-13). By their example, they were not to destroy the work of God in the hearts of his people, leading them to life with him. That work is too precious to be hindered in any way by fellow Christians. Their actions were to give witness to justice, peace, and a concern for one another's welfare. That will be evidence that Christ lives in them. Paul points out that the words of scripture are a source of encouragement for them in their witness. He prays that the Lord will enable the Romans to live up to this directive.

In what situations do these words speak to you?

____

____

Read Romans 15:14-21

Paul now concludes his long letter to the Romans. He explains his boldness by comparing his ministry to that of the priests of the Old Testament. As they offered gifts to God, so Paul offers the evangelized Gentiles as consecrated gifts to the Father. The image expresses the call that Paul experienced to minister to the Gentiles and the sacredness of his work. He knows that all his work is accomplished through the power of Christ.

How can this image of ministry apply to the work you do for the Lord?

___

___

Read Romans 15:22-33

Here Paul mentions some of the places he has worked and his plans for the future. It seems Paul always had plans, but they were subject to the plan of the Lord. Having preached in Asia and Greece, he intended to travel to Rome and even to Spain to proclaim the saving message of Christ. Paul knew that journeying to Jerusalem before coming to Rome would be risky. The unbelieving Jews were angry with him. He asks the Roman community to pray that he be kept safe. The supportive prayer of his people was important to Paul. As mentioned in the introduction, he is kept safe in Jerusalem, but not quite the way he had planned. He eventually arrives in Rome, but in the custody of a Roman guard. Paul will write the rest of his letters from Rome and will see his arrival there as part of God's plan for his life.

How do you submit your plans to the Lord?

___

___

Scholars seriously question whether or not Chapter 16 was part of Paul's original letter to the Romans. It contains a rather long list of people to greet in a community that Paul has never visited. From other sources, there is evidence that at least some of the people mentioned in this chapter lived in Ephesus. Perhaps it is part of a letter sent to the community there, which Paul knew very well. Whatever its destination, its origin is Paul and its contents contain his deep love for many people.

Read Romans 16:1-2
Paul briefly recommends Phoebe as he has recommended others. Her designation as deaconess seems to refer to a special religious group of the community of Cenchreae, near Corinth. She has been helpful to Paul and he hopes that she will be welcomed in her new location.

Read Romans 16:3-16
In his usual style, Paul sends warm greetings to people he knows. He has such a powerful way of affirming them! Apparently, he had engaged many different people in the work of the Lord. We get the impression that they mean very much to him.

What effect does being affirmed by someone you love have on you?

____

____

Read Romans 16:17-27
The warning contained here is quite different from the tone of the rest of this letter. It may well be a warning to the Ephesian community which, as Paul knew from experience, was plagued with many troublemakers. Paul gives the greetings of his coworkers in Corinth. Then Tertius, his scribe, adds his greeting. Paul ends with a word of praise to God the Father, through his son, Jesus Christ.

According to many scholars, the letter to the community at Rome has influenced later Christian theology more than any other New Testament book. Whatever its influence, we can see that it is filled with much teaching. It left the early church with some powerful statements concerning the gift of justification and the way to salvation. Whether or not Paul intended that is hard to say, but it seems clear that he would have been open to God using his words in any way that would bring glory to him.

Summary Question

What teaching of Paul in this letter has most influenced your life?

____

____

Questions for Reflection and Discussion

1. What teaching of Paul in this letter has most influenced your life?

2. How would you introduce yourself to a Christian community?

3. What spiritual benefits do you experience from sharing a common faith with someone?

4. What are some ways that a non-believer might come to experience God in creation?

5. How does the message of justification in Christ in Romans 3:21-31 strengthen you on the road to salvation?

6. In what ways do you feel the graced presence of Jesus strengthening you on your life journey?

7. Through what means do you experience the gift of God's reconciliation in your community?

8. How do you use Christ's power to overcome sin in your life?

9. What things can you do to gradually root out sin from your life?

10. What are your feelings as you reflect on God as a warm, loving "daddy"?

11. Describe a bad experience in which you were able to see God bring about some good?

12. In what ways can you identify with Paul's feelings about his ancestry?

13. How do you participate in building the "new Jerusalem"?

14. In what ways have you ever experienced the frustration of not being able to "force" someone to believe?

15. When do you take time to thank God for his awesome, saving mercy?

16. Which directive in Romans 12:1-21 speaks most to your heart?

17. In what situations do you feel that a Christian has the right or obligation to disobey his or her government?

18. In what situations does Romans 14:1 to 15:13 speak to you?

19. How can the image of ministry in Romans 15:14-21 apply to the work you do for the Lord?

20. How do you submit your plans to the Lord?

21. What effect does being affirmed by someone you love have on you?

Chapter 8

The Letter to Philemon

Father, you have gifted each of us in many ways. Through Christ you have given us the inner freedom of forgiveness. In him, you have united us as one. As we share in the words of this letter, help us to see your goodness in every person and every event. May we grow in acceptance of all people, and together praise you as Lord forever and ever. Amen.

The Letter to Philemon might more accurately be called a postcard. It is brief and unlike Paul's other letters thus far. It is addressed to one person rather than a community. The letter to Philemon was written by Paul while he was under house arrest in Rome from A.D. 61-63. It addresses a very specific situation, but contains a rather universal message.

Read Philemon, the whole letter

Do you get a feel for the situation? It is unique. Onesimus is Philemon's slave, who ran away after doing some harm to his owner. It seems Onesimus ends up in Rome, where Paul gives him refuge and converts him. When Paul learns that Onesimus legally belongs to Philemon, he decides to send him back to his owner. Paul writes this letter begging Philemon to receive him back "no longer as a slave . . . but as a brother . . . in the Lord." He tells Philemon not to inflict the severe penalty permitted by law. Paul sends Onesimus back with Tychicus (Colossians 4:7-9), to ensure that he would get there.

Read Philemon 1-16

Philemon was apparently one of Paul's co-workers (verses 1-7). Paul especially loved and prayed for those who helped him in the work of Christ. As friend and brother in Christ, Paul gently begins making his request of Philemon. He considers Onesimus his "child" because he has given him life in the Lord. The name Onesimus means "useful," and Paul plays on that word in verse 11. Paul says that he wants to keep Onesimus as a helper in Rome, but decides to ask the "consent" of Philemon, "that kindness might not be forced" on him. He knew he was going to make a heavy demand on Philemon and points out that there may have been some deeper purpose for the whole incident, namely, that Philemon and Onesimus might live forever as brothers in the Lord. Paul's vision of life is eternal.

How do you prepare people when you wish to make a request of them?

____

____

Read Philemon 17-25

Having prepared Philemon's heart, Paul makes his request (verse 17). Legally, Philemon could kill Onesimus, or scourge him, or brand him for running away. That he as master should accept him back as "brother" was more than a small favor. Paul says that he will pay for anything Onesimus owes. He is not afraid to show his love. Confidently, Paul then suggests that Philemon might free Onesimus to come and work with him in Rome (verses 20-21). Paul's request is based on the new relationship "in the Lord" that Christians share with one another.

Which people do you find hardest to accept as brothers and sisters in the Lord?

____

____

It is important to note that Paul makes no recommendation about the institution of slavery. He accepts it as part of his culture. He calls for renunciation on the part of slave and master based on their relationship in the Lord. Each of them is called to make a free decision for reconciliation on the strength of their life with Christ. To that extent, all Christians are able to find themselves in this letter.

Questions for Reflection and Discussion

1. How do you prepare people when you wish to make a request of them?

2. What kind of people do you find hardest to accept as brothers and sisters in the Lord?

Chapter 9

The Letter to the Colossians

Father, we praise and thank you for the gift of your son, Jesus. In him you have created all things, and through him you allow us to share in the joy of eternal life with you. May the words of this letter renew our life in him and empower us to clothe ourselves daily with his virtues. Whatever we do, whether in word or in action, may it be done in the name of Christ, your son, giving thanks and praise to you, Father, forever and ever. Amen.

The letter to the community at Colossae is written in response to some disturbing news Paul had received that certain false teachers were spreading their doctrines among the Christians there. Paul had not founded the community at Colossae, but he felt impelled to write to them and confront the false teachings. Like the letter to Philemon, it seems Paul wrote this letter during his house arrest in Rome (A.D. 61-63).

A few scholars raise the question as to whether or not Paul actually wrote this letter. Although the language, style, and theology of this letter differ somewhat from his earlier letters, there is no convincing evidence that it is not his work. Most scholars believe it is written by Paul.

Read Colossians 1:1-8

Paul greets the Colossian community in his usual way and

then goes on to affirm them for the way they are growing in faith. It seems that Epaphras, one of Paul's converts in Ephesus, took the message of the gospel to Colossae and founded the community there. Through contact with Epaphras, Paul feels close to the Colossians. They are his "grandchildren." He is grateful to God for them.

Read Colossians 1:9-12
Here Paul expresses his hopes for the Colossians. He prays that they will attain full knowledge of God's will, for then he knows that they will receive all his other gifts. With God's help, they will be able to "endure joyfully whatever may come." Paul is speaking from experience.

When you pray for people, for what do you pray?

____

____

This next section might be clearer if we understand the context of Paul's words. He is responding to some false doctrines being spread in Colossae, which held that certain angelic beings controlled human affairs and all of creation (Colossians 2:8, 18-23). Paul uses poetic words to stress the preeminence of Christ above all other beings.

Read Colossians 1:13-23
Paul's words about Christ are profound. He points out Christ's free redemptive actions (verses 13-14) and then uses what may be part of an early Christian hymn to expound on his unique supremacy over all creation (verses 15-20). In and through him all was created and continues in existence. He is head of the church. He shares in the absolute fullness of God and thus has the power to reconcile all of creation. Paul's words proclaim the preeminence of Christ over all and leave us aware that early Christians were growing in their understanding of Jesus. Christians throughout history would continually seek to comprehend and appreciate the magnificent person of Jesus Christ. Paul encourages the Colossians to do just that.

How would you describe Jesus Christ?

____

____

Read Colossians 1:24-2:3

Although Paul does not know the Colossians personally, he makes it known that they are part of him. Paul is suffering in prison, but he accepts it as a means of making the victory of Christ's suffering visible and effective in his time. He made every situation valuable by his vision of faith. He witnesses to the Colossians that the energy of Christ strengthens him in all his struggles. Through his struggles and prayers, he hopes that they will remain united in God's love.

Read Colossians 2:4-15

Paul hopes that his prayers and concern for the Christians at Colossae will keep them from being "deluded" by the false teachers in their midst. He encourages them to continue living in Christ, rooted in his life-giving love. Paul knew that the "seductive philosophy" based on "cosmic powers" did not have the redeeming and freeing power of Christ's love. In simple imagery, Paul reminds the Colossians that in baptism they died to sin in order to receive the gift of new life from God. Through Christ, they share in the victory over all other cosmic powers. Paul's words left a message for Christians of all time.

What are some philosophies or teachings today that attribute "power" to cosmic signs?

____

____

Read Colossians 2:16-3:4

In these verses, Paul alludes to another apparently false teaching, namely, that the Christians were required to follow Jewish customs and observances (verse 16). Paul makes it clear that those things are past. As Christians "raised up in the company of Christ," Paul tells the Colossians to fix their attention on the will of God, not on earthly philosophies or old observances. They had been "created anew" and Paul wants them to live in the freedom and peace of their new life in Christ. He could not stand to see them "robbed" of that gift.

Read Colossians 3:5-17

Having spoken his mind about the threatening heresies, Paul goes on to remind the Colossians of how they, as Christians, were to live. His words are demanding. They sound like an early baptismal instruction, using the imagery of "putting aside" the old and "putting on" the new. Paul expects much of "regular people," yet he was always patient and gentle with them. He knows from experience that the process of transformation in Christ takes time. His words give the community of Colossae a beautiful summary of his vision. His vision gives the church one of the most profound descriptions of Christian virtue. It remains for us to make it our own.

Read Colossians 3:18-21

The directives that Paul gives to family members will best be understood if we can feel the power of his phrase, "in the Lord." Paul uses that phrase in his later letters (Philemon, Colossians, and Ephesians) to designate the new relationship that Christians share because they are one in Christ. Recall that it is on the basis of that relationship that Paul asks Philemon to welcome back his slave. He now asks family members, as one in the Lord, to relate to each other in a way worthy of their new relationship. As we have seen in his letter to the Corinthians (1 Corinthians 7:1-9), Paul calls both wives and husbands to model themselves on the self-sacrificing love of Christ. His demands for loyalty and true love are fulfilled through the power flowing from Christ and the couples' relationship "in him." Paul points out that Christian children are no longer related to their parents just by blood; they are also related "in the Lord." On the basis of that new relationship, children must obey their parents. By this time in his life, Paul had truly come to know the power flowing from being one with Christ. As Christians would come to feel that power, his words would become a reality in their homes.

How does your relationship with the Lord affect your relationship with your family?

____

____

Read Colossians 3:22-4:1
Paul's directives for Christian slaves and slaveowners are given with the vision that all share the same master. Both were to be distinguished by their witness of Christian virtues. Paul knows that real freedom cannot be forced. It comes from accepting Jesus as Lord and master. In him, masters and slaves are equal. As Christians throughout history proclaimed their true equality by their witness, the institution of slavery would gradually crumble.

Read Colossians 4:2-6
Paul tells his people to stand fast in prayer. Again he asks for the prayers of other Christians, aware of the power of their unified voice before God. As a loving "grandfather" he gives them a few concluding words of advice.

How have you experienced the supporting power of prayer?

____

____

Read Colossians 4:7-14
Paul's final words in his letter leave us little bits of historical information. Between the lines, we feel Paul's love for his coworkers and his concern for all Christians. As pointed out earlier, verses 7-9 tell us that Tychicus accompanied Onesimus back to Philemon, his owner. The other names mentioned here are very similar to the ones listed in the conclusion to Paul's letter to Philemon (verses 23-24), indicating the same place of writing. Apparently. Epaphras, the founder of the Colossian

community, as well as Mark and Luke, two of the gospel writers, were all in Rome at this time.

Read Colossians 4:15-18

These words of Paul indicate that local communities began to circulate his letters. They were read when the community assembled, as Christian churches still do today. The letter coming from Laodicea, a nearby town, seems to be the one that came to be known as the letter to the Ephesians. Paul ends with his personal greeting and a request for the Colossians to pray for him in his imprisonment.

How do you think the people would have received Paul's words as they were read in the assembly?

____

____

In this letter, Paul has warned the Colossians and other Christians about the false teachers and has reaffirmed for them the power and supremacy of Jesus Christ. Out of concern and love, he told them how they were to live their new life "in the Lord." His words remain a rich treasure to all who seek to follow Christ.

Summary Question

What message in this letter is most challenging to you?

____

____

Questions for Reflection and Discussion

1. What message in this letter is most challenging to you?

2. When you pray for people, for what do you pray?

3. How would you describe Jesus Christ?

4. What are some philosophies or teachings today that attribute "power" to cosmic signs?

5. How does your relationship with the Lord affect your relationship with your family?

6. How have you experienced the supporting power of prayer?

7. How do you think the people would have received Paul's words in Colossians 4:15-18 as they were read in the assembly?

Chapter 10

The Letter to the Ephesians

Father, you have beautifully fashioned your plan of salvation for all of us. Because of your generous love for us, you have brought us to life in Christ. As we reflect on your word, may we grow in appreciation of that gift. May his power within us transform our lives, and may his Spirit fashion us into more genuine witnesses of your love. We make our prayer through Christ our life forever and ever. Amen.

The Letter to the Ephesians seems to have been written for a number of Christian communities around Ephesus. Its lack of personal references to community members, as usually seen in Paul's letters, and the fact that the title "to the Ephesians" was not on the original letter, lead us to believe that it was addressed to more than one Christian community. This letter could well have been written to our community, for it contains a beautiful vision of God's plan of salvation being brought about in Christ. In it we find a precious summary of Paul's thoughts as they have developed through his years of ministry.

There are quite a few scholars who question whether or not Paul actually wrote this letter. Its style (i.e., long, complex sentences) is quite different from any of Paul's other letters.

Another fact noted by scholars is that over one-third of the 155 verses in Ephesians are parallel to Paul's letter to the Colossians in their content and order. Paul is usually more creative than that. If Paul did not write this letter, however, he certainly must have commissioned one of his co-workers to do it, since it contains a rich development of his thoughts. In that sense, it is "Paul's letter." That commissioning probably occurred shortly after Paul wrote to the Colossians (A.D. 61-63) from Rome.

Read Ephesians 1:1-2

Paul's greeting is short. As mentioned earlier, the words "at Ephesus" were not on the original letter. Each community that received the letter could insert its own name. We find expressed in the first verse Paul's constant awareness that it is "by the will of God" that he is an apostle.

How often do you remind yourself that it is by God's favor that you are who you are?

____

____

Read Ephesians 1:3-14

These verses form a hymn summarizing Paul's vision of God's saving plan. It begins by praising God for his rich blessings bestowed in Christ. From all eternity his plan was to form a holy people full of love. The predestination mentioned here is not individual; it is rather a community of all who are immersed in the presence of God through Christ. The hymn emphasizes the central redeeming role of Christ in bringing all creation into one, as a gift of praise to the Father (see Colossians 1:15-20). Both Jews (verse 11) and Gentiles (verse 13) share in God's blessings by their faith in Christ, sealed with the Holy Spirit. Having read most of Paul's letters by now, we can appreciate how beautifully this hymn draws together many of his thoughts on the generous saving plan of God. What a treasure it is!

Can you recall some of the places in Paul's letters where he wrote about the themes mentioned here?

____

____

Read Ephesians 1:15-23
Here Paul prays that the Ephesians, and all who read this letter, will come to know the vision that God holds for each of them as part of the church. He wants all Christians to know the "immeasurable scope of God's power" in them to carry out his plan for their lives. Paul has been sustained by that power, which raised Jesus from the dead. He knew that it was available for all who accepted the message of resurrection.

Read Ephesians 2:1-10
Contrasting human weakness with the divine plan of salvation, Paul accents the rich, saving mercy of God. He uses the word "rich" five times in this letter to describe the abundance of God's mercy. Who was more aware than Paul that it was by God's favor that he had life? He had been spiritually dead until he met Christ on the road to Damascus. Paul powerfully shares with the Ephesians that saving message, showing them that by their faith they too are on the road of "life." All of them are the "handiwork" of God, "regular people" redeemed by his rich mercy expressed in Christ, and called to live a life of good deeds until they arrive at final salvation in him. We can rejoice to be in that number and feel grateful that our God is abundant in showing love.

How do you express your gratitude for God's rich mercy to you?

____

____

Read Ephesians 2:11-22
Using a number of images, Paul shows the Gentiles and the

Jews of these early communities how God has formed them into one. Through the cross of Christ, the old barriers have been abolished. The Gentiles who were "far off" and the Jews who were "near" have been created anew as one community in Christ. Paul had spent his life to help bring about this unity that he envisioned, and now these Christian communities stood as a witness that his effort was worthwhile. Thoughts of them must have brought tears to his eyes. They probably still had their differences, but he believed that by the power of the Holy Spirit dwelling among them, they would "take shape as a holy temple in the Lord."

How do you see the Spirit of God breaking down barriers today within Christian communities?

____

____

Read Ephesians 3:1-13

Not all of the Christians knew Paul; therefore, he describes how he sees himself fitting into God's plan of salvation. He again humbly admits that it is out of God's goodness that he became a minister of the gospel. As the "least of all believers," he was chosen to preach the "unfathomable riches of Christ" and to help reveal God's saving plan. All the Christians, as one church, were now chosen to continue his work. Paul assures them that in Christ they can speak to God freely, drawing near to him as a child does to a father, confident of his abiding love. That was Paul's source of strength and peace. He now shares it with those who will carry on the work of Christ.

In what ways do you tell others of the saving love of God?

____

____

Read Ephesians 3:14-21
Feel the eloquent strength of this prayer! Paul kneels in prison before the Lord, whom he has come to know as Father, and prays for all who would read his letter. He says it all in one prayer. Stop and reflect on the power of his words.

Who in your life might be strengthened by your praying in a similar way for them?

____

____

Read Ephesians 4:1-6
In the remainder of this letter, Paul gives some directives for Christian conduct. We have heard many of these words in previous letters, but as God's word, they are always refreshing. Paul begins by pleading with his people to live a life worthy of their calling, manifesting the attitudes of Christ. He then encourages them to preserve the unity that has the Spirit as its origin. In a unique sevenfold formula, Paul accents the oneness that Christians share in God. This letter, more than any other of Paul's letters, speaks of Christian unity.

Read Ephesians 4:7-13
Within the basic unity, there are a variety of gifts and offices, each given by God for a specific purpose. In Paul's vision, God gave the offices of apostles, prophets, evangelists, and pastor-teachers "to equip the saints for the work of ministries." These spiritual leaders are to equip all believers to do Christ's work. Paul has trained Christians to use their unique gifts for Christ, and now he encourages other Christian leaders to do the same.

How do the leaders in your community equip you to do Christ's ministry?

____

____

Read Ephesians 4:14-16
Paul briefly tells his people not to fall prey to any more false teachers. Again he stresses their unity in Christ and the power of his abiding love.

Read Ephesians 4:17-5:2
With words he used earlier (Galatians 5:13-16; Colossians 3:1-17), Paul calls the Christians around Ephesus to live a morally good life. They must put aside the old ways and put on the new ways of Christ. Paul expands on what he means. They must stop lying and stealing. They are to resolve their anger in a way that will not harm themselves or someone else. Their speech is to be upbuilding, lest they grieve God's Spirit by injuring someone in whom he dwells. They must let go of all that is deadly within them, forgiving as Christ has forgiven them. In kindness, compassion, and forgiveness, they are to imitate God.

Read Ephesians 5:3-20
Paul continues his exhortation, pointing out actions that he feels are not in keeping with the Christian way of life. He wants his people to live as children of the light, trying to discern the will of the Lord for their lives. Their Christian joy was to result not from being drunk on wine, but from being totally immersed in the Holy Spirit. In the joy of that Spirit, they would give praise and thanks to God.

This entire exhortation (4:17-5:20) would form the basis for much moral teaching in the Christian church. It expands on Jesus' teaching, yet it can be summed up in his two great commandments. Christians are left to help one another make these teachings a reality in their lives.

Read Ephesians 5:21-33
This section sounds very much like Paul's words to husbands and wives in his letter to the Colossians (3:18-19). Here Christian marriage is seen as a symbol of the intimate love relationship between Christ and his church. Using that parallel, Paul again stresses the self-sacrificing love that must characterize a marriage in the Lord. Paul envisioned the authority in a Christian marriage coming through the husband, but his demand on the husband tc minister that authority in love is equally as difficult as the demand on the wife to receive it with loyalty. His directives were possible with the help of Christ. Christian mar-

riages that genuinely demonstrated selfless love and loyal respect continued throughout history to proclaim that Christ was among his people. They remain a living sign of Christ's abiding love.

How has Christ spoken to you through a marriage that you have seen or experienced?

___

___

Read Ephesians 6:1-9

This section parallels Colossians 3:20-4:1 very closely. The conduct in the home must be based on the family's new relationship "in the Lord." As equal before the Lord, slaves and masters were called to turn their attention to their common master.

Read Ephesians 6:10-17

On occasion, Paul has spoken of "putting on" the virtues of Christ, but he has never mentioned putting on armor. He has encouraged his people to "stand firm," but never in reference to the "tactics of the devil." In fact, this is the only place in the New Testament where that phrase is found. In that sense, these verses do not sound quite like Paul, yet the encouragement given is definitely based on the strength of the Lord. To anyone who ever saw a Roman soldier, the imagery would be clear. With the Lord's help, Christians had the necessary equipment to withstand any enemy.

What means do you use to "fight off" temptations in your life?

___

___

Read Ephesians 6:18-24

Paul encourages his fellow Christians to pray for one another at every opportunity. He requested the prayer support of the whole communion of believers that he might courageously carry out his mission in the face of impending death. There is no list of greetings that Paul usually includes when writing to a specific community. He simply mentions that Tychicus, his co-worker, is bringing news of his condition. Paul does give his blessing to all who will assemble in their communities and listen to the words he has written.

How does your community profit by the power of communal prayer?

____

____

While the Letter to Ephesians does not have the personal touch of some of Paul's earlier letters, it does contain his richest thoughts on God's plan of salvation and the meaning of that plan for Christians. It does not portray the deep feelings of Paul, but it says much of the rich mercy of God. Another person may have written this letter, but it is Paul's life witness and deep faith that gives power to its words.

Summary Question

Which people that you know speak powerfully because of the way they live?

____

____

Questions for Reflection and Discussion

1. Which people that you know speak powerfully because of the way they live?

2. How often do you remind yourself that it is by God's favor that you are who you are?

3. Can you recall some of the places in Paul's letters where he wrote about the themes mentioned in Ephesians 1:3-14?

4. How do you express your gratitude for God's rich mercy to you?

5. How do you see the Spirit of God breaking down barriers today within Christian communities?

6. In what ways do you tell others of the saving love of God?

7. Who in your life might be strengthened by your praying for them in a way similar to Ephesians 3:14-21?

8. How do the leaders in your community equip you to do Christ's ministry?

9. How has Christ spoken to you through a marriage that you have seen or experienced?

10. What means do you use to "fight off" temptations in your life?

11. How does your community profit by the power of communal prayer?

Chapter 11

The First Letter to Timothy

Father, we are grateful for your gift of life and for the many people you place along our life journey. We thank you for friends and for those who guide us in our Christian faith. Help us as we grow in knowledge of your word to accept the ministry to which you call us. By our love and encouragement, may we affirm our Christian leaders and those aspiring to leadership in the name of your son. Together may we bring others to know the fullness of your love which you radiate upon us now and forever. Amen.

Paul's last three letters are addressed to two of his disciples, Timothy and Titus, whom we have come to know through his earlier letters (see 1 Corinthians 4:17; Galatians 2:1; 2 Corinthians 7:5-7 and 8:16-23). Following Paul's house arrest in Rome, it seems he made a journey to Ephesus and Crete, establishing Timothy and Titus respectively as "bishops" of those communities. Paul then writes these "pastoral letters" (1 Timothy, Titus, and 2 Timothy) to direct his co-workers in their leadership duties. These last letters seem to be written around A.D. 65-67, during the last years of Paul's life. Some scholars suggest that Paul did not write these letters. The evidence relating to this issue is scanty and inconclusive. You will have to make your own judgment. They sound like Paul to me.

In his first letter to Timothy, Paul stresses the need for the community to hold on to the deposit of faith that was handed on to them, lest it be corrupted by false teaching. He also gives some qualities that should be evident in the lives of those who take on Christian leadership.

Read 1 Timothy 1:1-2

Paul establishes his authority as an apostle and then confirms the authority of Timothy. Paul had brought Timothy to know Christ in his first missionary journey (c. A.D. 47) and he loved him as his own child.

Read 1 Timothy 1:3-11

As new pastor of the Ephesian community, Timothy was called to guard the people against false teachings. As the church continued to grow, it was very important to hold on to true faith, as faith could easily be influenced and redefined by other teachings. Apparently, teachings about myths and the law were prevalent in Ephesus, and Paul instructs Timothy to keep his people safe from such influences.

In what ways does your community discern and guard against false teachings?

____

____

Read 1 Timothy 1:12-17

Paul becomes distracted in his directives to Timothy and gives a very powerful witness of Christ's mercy to him. He is not afraid to mention his former life because he is absolutely confident that in Christ he has been forgiven. By his experience of forgiveness in Christ, he assures all believers of God's abundant mercy and gentle patience. He praises God for such goodness.

What message comes to you from these verses?

Read 1 Timothy 1:18-20
It seems that prophecies directed the choice of Timothy as pastor of the Ephesian community, and Paul encourages him to remain strong in the power of their inspiration. Paul then mentions that he turned some false teachers "over to Satan." Recall in 1 Corinthians 5:5 that the excommunication of the sinner was a punishment meant to eventually lead a person to a renewed life.

Read 1 Timothy 2:1-15
Paul gives some directives for men and women regarding their community prayer gatherings. He tells them to pray for everyone, especially leaders, since he continues to be convinced that God plans to bring all people to himself. Paul's instructions regarding men's and women's gestures during prayer reflect his Jewish background and the customs of the larger church (1 Corinthians 14:26-40). His Jewish heritage is evident, but his acceptance and concern for all people are also visible. He calls both men and women "similarly" to be in the right attitude of heart when they pray.

How do you put yourself into a disposition for prayer?

Read 1 Timothy 3:1-7
In these verses, Paul gives a list of qualities that should be evident in those who aspire to leadership positions in the Christian community. What Paul describes here as a "bishop" would be somewhat equivalent to what we refer to today as a priest

or pastor. Our current distinctions of church leaders developed from these beginnings to fit the needs of the growing church. The qualifications mentioned for bishops gave Timothy an example of what to look for in selecting leaders. Those who would guide others in their faith journey had to reflect the attitudes that flow from a life immersed in the Spirit of God. They were to have gifts to teach and manage people within the community. Through God's continued gift of such qualities to Christians, he would guide the church.

Read 1 Timothy 3:8-13
As caretakers of charitable funds and assistants in the guidance of the community, deacons were to have qualities similar to bishops. They particularly had to be free from greed because they distributed church funds. There is no way of telling whether or not the women mentioned in verse 11 refer to deaconesses or to wives of the deacons. The qualities Paul describes in these verses could almost be applied to every Christian. All are called to be servants of the Lord.

What are the qualities that help you serve Christ in your everyday life?

____

____

Read 1 Timothy 3:14-4:11
Paul hopes to visit Timothy, but indicates that his plans may be delayed. He tells Timothy to continue giving the Ephesian community sound teaching, that they might not be led astray by "men with seared consciences." With a little play on words, Paul instructs Timothy to "exercise" himself in piety, for it will keep him healthy in the Lord. Through the words of verse 10, Paul again manifests his vision that in some way, by God's goodness, all people will be brought to final salvation.

Read 1 Timothy 4:12-16
In a few brief verses, Paul encourages his disciple Timothy to persevere in giving good example and doing the work of minis-

try. The laying on of hands was a gesture used in the early Christian communities to confer a church office or leadership role. Apparently, Paul and a group of presbyters (pastors) laid hands on Timothy before he took his leadership position. Paul reminds Timothy not to neglect the gift he received, when through this gesture he was "ordained" for that work. These verses give much on which to reflect.

Read 1 Timothy 5:1-16

Paul begins this section by comparing the Christian community to a large family. Members are to treat each other with respect and love. That love is to be extended especially to the needy, such as widows who have no one to care for them. Paul gives some simple directives as to how the church was to minister to them. In verses 9-15, he makes reference to a constituted order of widows who apparently dedicated themselves to charitable works. Paul indicates that this group was for elderly widows. His reasons show a realistic understanding of human nature. This entire section contains a wealth of common sense.

In your community, what groups care for needs similar to those mentioned in these verses?

____

____

Read 1 Timothy 5:17-25

The word Paul uses here (presbyter) refers to the same office that he termed bishop in chapter three. He uses the words interchangeably. He says that such church leaders should be paid according to their work. He tells Timothy to give his pastors special protection against false charges, but if one should commit an offense, he is to publicly rebuke him. Timothy is to be careful who he "ordains" as spiritual leaders because they carry great responsibilities. Paul then gives his disciple some practical medical advice. Throughout this chapter, we see Paul's concern that all goes well with Timothy and the people in his care. Paul's love and advice are endless.

Read 1 Timothy 6:1-2
Paul's directives to slaves stress the power of their good witness. By their respect and service they can benefit all who see them.

Read 1 Timothy 6:3-10
In this section, Paul again warns against false teachers. He indicates that many of them were desiring material gain. Paul says that such a desire is deadly and had already destroyed some Christians. His words in verses 7-8 indicate his own attitude of selflessness, which we have seen throughout his life. For him, the Christian communities were his pay, and life with the Father was his security.

How do you wrestle with the human desire for material goods?

____

____

Read 1 Timothy 6:11-16
In a profound yet simple way, Paul tells Timothy to be rich in the fruits of the Spirit (Galatians 5:22). He charges him to hold to the deposit of faith entrusted to him by God, that it might be unstained until Christ's final coming.

Read 1 Timothy 6:17-21
In his final words, Paul again expresses his vision of real security and his concern for Timothy to guard the true message of faith. He ends with a wish for the whole community. He knew that his disciple would share these words with all of them.

This letter leaves us with Paul's vision of Christian leadership and the responsibilities of that task. It makes all the "regular people" of the Christian communities aware of the awesome responsibilities carried by their leaders. It allows all of us to reflect on our part in teaching and preaching, by word and example, the true message of the gospel.

Questions for Reflection and Discussion

1. In what ways does your community discern and guard against false teachings?

2. What message comes to you from 1 Timothy 1:12-17?

3. How do you put yourself into a disposition for prayer?

4. What are the qualities that help you serve Christ in your everyday life?

5. In your community, what groups care for needs similar to those mentioned in 1 Timothy 5:1-16?

6. How do you wrestle with the human desire for material goods?

Chapter 12

The Letter to Titus

Father, your word enlightens our minds and warms our hearts. Through it we come to know the scope of your abundant mercy and the life to which you call each of us. Anoint us with your Spirit as we search for your will and seek to live according to your plan. May our efforts help bring your plan to completion and all people to life with you forever and ever. Amen.

The Letter to Titus is written around the same time as Paul's first letter to Timothy (A.D. 65-67) and contains many similar instructions. As mentioned in the introduction to that letter, it is one of the pastoral letters. This letter is addressed to Paul's disciple, Titus, who was appointed administrator of the Christian communities on the island of Crete. Titus had apparently known Paul for a long time (Galatians 2:1) and had helped him in his ministry, especially to the Corinthian community (2 Corinthians 7:5-7; 8:16-23).

Read Titus 1:1-4

Perhaps assuming that his letter will be read to all the communities in Crete, Paul begins by introducing himself. He acknowledges his commission to preach the gospel message, and then as he did with Timothy, he confirms the authority of Titus.

Read Titus 1:5-9

This section is parallel to 1 Timothy 3:1-7. As we have seen, Paul uses the words "presbyter" and "bishop" interchangeably to designate an office which is similar to what we call "pastor" or "priest." The main task of Titus in Crete was to appoint a "presbyter-bishop" in every town to care for the newly established Christian communities. The qualities of these "presbyter-bishops" are listed with a final emphasis on their need to hold fast to the authentic message of faith. The leaders of these Christian communities had to be able to refute any false teaching that might be spread in these remote localities.

How do you think Titus went about carrying out this task?

____

____

Read Titus 1:10-16

We get the impression that Paul was upset with a group of false teachers in Crete. He uses some rather strong words to describe them, and makes it clear to Titus that he is to admonish them. Paul's dedication to his calling as an apostle makes him very protective of his people. He invested himself totally in bringing others to the freedom of life in Christ, and he has no kind words for those who destroyed that life.

Can you recall other occasions when Paul showed his feelings like this?

____

____

Read Titus 2:1-15

Paul gives Titus an assortment of directives, similar to those he gave Timothy. The older members of the community are to teach the younger ones, and together all are to live a life witness exemplifying their oneness with God. Through the sacrifice of Christ, they have been redeemed and empowered to live their new lives. In expressing the hope found in their "great God and Savior Jesus Christ," Paul leaves us an eloquent expression of his belief in the divinity of Christ. All these things Titus is to teach with authority and confidence.

Read Titus 3:1-8a

Titus has probably heard Paul use the words and expressions of these verses in other Christian communities. Here Paul is telling Titus to remind his people of these teachings. Verses 4-7 again reflect Paul's deep awareness that it is out of God's kindness and love that Christians are made right with their creator. Through the Holy Spirit received at baptism, Christians have the power to transform their lives and inherit the gift of eternal life. Paul again proclaims God's greatest gift and shows how we share in it. He could never proclaim it enough!

How do you proclaim God's gift of redemption?

____

____

Read Titus 3:8b-15

Paul's closing advice is very straightforward and uncompromising. Like a father talking to his son, Paul gives Titus some final words, hoping that he will guard the true message of the gospel from error. Paul hopes to see Titus again at Nicopolis after Artemas or Tychicus replaces him in Crete. The final greeting indicates the love that united Paul and his people.

How would you deal with a "false teacher" if you found yourself talking with one?

____

____

In these few chapters God's message of salvation has been proclaimed. Paul's letter to Titus is brief. He did not have to say much to a man who worked with him so long. Titus knew the "letter" himself. He knew Paul well and could probably have told us the things he would say. For us, however, this letter adds yet another piece to our picture of Paul and reassures us of the message he spoke. We have one more piece to discover.

Questions for Reflection and Discussion

1. How do you think Titus went about carrying out his task in Titus 1:5-9?

2. Can you recall other occasions when Paul showed his feelings as he does in Titus 1:10-16?

3. How do you proclaim God's gift of redemption?

4. How would you deal with a "false teacher" if you found yourself talking with one?

Chapter 13

The Second Letter to Timothy

Father, we praise and bless you for the depth of your love and for your many servants who exemplify that love. Through Paul's words and example, you have gifted us with a true witness of love. We thank you for all who bring your message of mercy and compassion to us each day. May your word, in all its richness, always find a home in our hearts and empower us to exemplify your love to others. We make all our prayers through Jesus, your son, who lives with you in the union of the Spirit now and forever. Amen.

Paul leaves us his last words in this Second Letter to Timothy. He has been imprisoned again and this time he knows that his death is imminent. He writes to his friend, his closest disciple, not because he has forgotten to tell him anything, but because he needs to share his heart with someone. As one of the pastoral letters, this letter contains some directives for Timothy, but its main content is the loving person that it reveals.

Read 2 Timothy 1:1-5
In his usual style, Paul introduces himself and greets his disciple. This time he expresses his love. He prays in gratitude for Timothy, and through his prayer, indicates the continuity he sees between his Jewish faith and the Christian message. He

has come to know that the God of his forebearers is the loving Father whom he now worships through Jesus, his son. Paul then indicates his pain in leaving Timothy in Ephesus. Paul's preaching of the gospel led to his imprisonment in Rome, from where he apparently writes this letter just before his death (c. A.D. 67). He hopes to see Timothy again.

Read 2 Timothy 1:6-14
In simple imagery, Paul gives some powerful encouragement to a man who seems somewhat timid. Paul knew the strength, love, and wisdom that flowed from God's Spirit. He wishes those things for the man who would carry on his work and share in the hardships of preaching the gospel. In his usual eloquent style, Paul summarizes the greatest act of God's love made manifest in Christ for the redemption of all who believe. Paul witnesses to his deep trust in God and through that witness calls Timothy to guard the rich message of faith that he has received. Paul is confident that with the help of God's Spirit, Timothy would live up to this task.

What do you think were Paul's greatest strengths for spreading the gospel message?

____

____

Read 2 Timothy 1:15-18
It appears that when Paul was arrested this last time for proclaiming the gospel, some of his fellow Christians did not help defend him. He is very grateful to Onesiphorus, who was courageous and concerned enough to visit Paul in prison and give him new spirit.

Read 2 Timothy 2:1-7
Timothy must be sure to hand on the truths of the faith to "trustworthy men" in order that the people may not be led astray. Knowing the "hardships which the gospel entails," Paul encourages Timothy to keep his eyes on Christ. He uses three familiar comparisons to emphasize the singleness of purpose

that Timothy should possess in proclaiming the gospel. He leaves words for all of us to reflect upon.

Read 2 Timothy 2: 8-13

These verses express the depth of Paul's faith in the resurrection and the power of God. People could imprison and chain the apostle to the Gentiles, but Paul knew that no power in heaven or on earth could "chain the word of God." He knew that his trusting acceptance of his destiny was a powerful proclamation to God's chosen ones that real life was eternal. His life witness continues to proclaim that message.

What actions in your life proclaim your belief in eternal life?

____

____

Read 2 Timothy 2:14-21

Paul tells Timothy to work at keeping his people from becoming mixed up in false teachings and worldly philosophies. Whatever the nature of these teachings, Christians were to avoid them, putting their full energy into living according to God's way. Apparently, Hymenaeus and Philetus denied the future resurrection of the body and eternal life. This upset some people, but Paul is confident that those founded on the Lord will stand firm through this incident. Paul uses the image of vessels within a household to reaffirm his message for Christians to stay clear of false teachings.

Read 2 Timothy 2:22-26

Paul directs some words to Timothy asking him to be an example of integrity, faith, love, and peace. He is to be patient and gentle with those who contradict him, with the hope that they might repent and turn to God. Paul's expectations of Timothy are high, but Paul knows the transforming power of God's Spirit. He has hopes that Timothy's life would increasingly manifest the fruits of that Spirit.

Which of these virtues do you most seek to imitate?

____

____

Read 2 Timothy 3:1-9
Here Paul reveals his vision of what will happen in the final days before the second coming of Christ. He indicates that some of those things were already happening. Paul has not spoken much about Christ's second coming since his earlier letter to the Thessalonians. Here he indicates that the present moral decay and false teachings may be evidence that this event is not far off.

Read 2 Timothy 3:10-17
Timothy knew many of Paul's persecutions because he had accompanied Paul on his journeys. Paul sees persecution as an inevitable part of living a "godly life in Christ Jesus." He tells Timothy to be faithful to the truths that he learned from childhood as a Jew and later came to understand in a new way through belief in Christ. Paul felt the power of scripture and believed that it was "inspired of God." He had used it much to correct and train his people. His "scripture" was what we know today as the Old Testament. After the New Testament was written, Christians applied Paul's words to the whole bible. Paul would have been awed and honored to think that his letters to the communities he loved would someday be considered "inspired of God" on the basis of this statement. He did not intend to include his words. Any of us, however, who have felt the power of God in his words, or experienced the change that the message of the gospel can make in one's life, have living proof that the entire scripture is inspired by God.

How do you absorb the power of God through his word?

____

____

Read 2 Timothy 4:1-5

In dramatic style, Paul charges Timothy to persist in preaching the word of God. He is aware that with time, people will be attracted by teachings that "tickle their ears." Paul knows from experience that people would look for an easier message. While they might find teachings that "sound good," they would never find a more life-giving message than that which came from Jesus Christ.

What are some of the teachings that "tickle people's ears" today?

____

____

Read 2 Timothy 4:6-8

Paul indicates here that his life is near the end. If anyone has "fought the good fight" of faith, he has. He has been freed from the fear of death by the saving message of Christ, which he has so faithfully proclaimed. He is ready to meet his creator. His life journey, his race, nears its end, and the way he approaches the finish line tells us that his race has not been in vain. In profound confidence, he now hands on his gift of faith and asks his beloved disciple, and us, to carry it with love.

Read 2 Timothy 4: 9-18

While Paul is confident of his reward, he still feels the human pain of loneliness. He requests Timothy to join him in Rome if he can. On his way, he is to pick up Mark, another of Paul's coworkers, and some important items left behind in Troas. Paul then warns Timothy about Alexander, who apparently had him arrested for his preaching. Paul is not angry with those who were too afraid to remain with him at that time. He continues to rely on the strength of the Lord that he is confident will keep him "safe" until he arrives in his heavenly home. Paul's faith and trust are undying.

Read 2 Timothy 4:19-22
Paul gives his final greetings and this time, they are final. He mentions Prisca and Aquila, who played a great role in his missionary activity (1 Corinthians 16:19; Romans 16:3-5). After his greetings, he again begs Timothy to come, if possible, and then wishes him the presence of the Lord. We do not know if Timothy made it to Rome to see Paul. We can be quite sure that together they did come to "see the Lord eternally."

Paul's second letter to Timothy contains some significant words and some deep feelings. In it Paul instructs his disciple and manifests his faith. His words give us his final thoughts and feelings. His faith and trust give all Christians an eternal hope and confidence.

Questions for Reflection and Discussion

1. What do you think were Paul's greatest strengths for spreading the gospel message?

2. What actions in your life proclaim your belief in eternal life?

3. Which of the virtues in 2 Timothy 2:22-26 do you most seek to imitate?

4. How do you absorb the power of God through his word?

5. What are some of the teachings that "tickle people's ears" today as they do in 2 Timothy 4:1-5?

Epilogue

This book has been written for "regular people," but by now you have come to know that you are all "holy, consecrated, anointed, and chosen people" through the abundant love of God.

In these pages, I have shared with you the thoughts and reflections that I have learned and heard from the Lord. Together we have journeyed with Paul. Along the way, we have heard his words, and through his words, the Word of God. Along the way, we have felt his love, and through his love, the love of God. We are "regular people" created anew by God. Through his rich mercy, we are holy in his sight, consecrated through his son, anointed with his Spirit, and chosen to proclaim his message of abiding love. Paul has told us this, and for this we are grateful.

As you journey forth in God's love, I pray with Paul that the Father

> will bestow on you gifts in keeping with the riches of his glory. May he strengthen you inwardly through the working of his Spirit. May Christ dwell in your hearts through

faith, and may charity be the root and foundation of your life. Thus you will be able to grasp fully, with all the holy ones, the breadth and length and height and depth of Christ's love, and experience this love which surpasses all knowledge, so that you may attain to the fullness of God himself. To him whose power now at work in us can do immeasurably more than we ask or imagine—to him be glory in the church and in Christ Jesus through all generations, world without end. Amen (Ephesians 3:16-21).

Sunday Readings

From Saint Paul's Letters

Cycle A

1st Sunday of Advent	Rom 13:11-14
2nd Sunday of Advent	Rom 15:4-9
4th Sunday of Advent	Rom 1:1-7
Christmas	Ti 2:11-14
Christmas	Ti. 3:4-7
Holy Family	Col 3:12-21
Octave of Christmas	Gal. 4:4-7
2nd Sunday after Christmas	Eph 1:3-6, 15-18
Epiphany	Eph 3:2-3, 5-6
1st Sunday of Lent	Rom 5:12-19
2nd Sunday of Lent	Tm 1:8-10
3rd Sunday of Lent	Rom 5:1-2, 5-8
4th Sunday of Lent	Eph 5:8-14
5th Sunday of Lent	Rom 8:8-11
Passion Sunday	Phil 2:6-11
Holy Thursday	1 Cor 11:23-26
Easter Vigil	Rom 6:3-11
Easter Sunday	1 Cor. 6:6-8 or Col. 3:12-21
Ascension	Eph 1:17-23
Pentecost Vigil	Rom 8:22-27
Pentecost Sunday	1 Cor 12:3-7, 12-13
2nd Sunday of the Year	1 Cor 1:1-3
3rd Sunday of the Year	1 Cor 1:10-13, 17
4th Sunday of the Year	1 Cor 1:26-31
5th Sunday of the Year	1 Cor 2:1-5
6th Sunday of the Year	1 Cor 2:6-10
7th Sunday of the Year	1 Cor 3:16-23
8th Sunday of the Year	1 Cor 4:1-5
9th Sunday of the Year	Rom 3:21-25, 28

10th Sunday of the Year	Rom 4:18-25
11th Sunday of the Year	Rom 5:6-11
12th Sunday of the Year	Rom 5:12-15
13th Sunday of the Year	Rom 6:3-4, 8-11
14th Sunday of the Year	Rom 8:9, 11-13
15th Sunday of the Year	Rom 8:18-23
16th Sunday of the Year	Rom 8:26-27
17th Sunday of the Year	Rom 8:28-30
18th Sunday of the Year	Rom 8:35, 37-39
19th Sunday of the Year	Rom 9:1-5
20th Sunday of the Year	Rom 11:13-15, 29-32
21st Sunday of the Year	Rom 11:33-36
22nd Sunday of the Year	Rom 12:1-2
23rd Sunday of the Year	Rom 13:8-10
24th Sunday of the Year	Rom 14:7-9
25th Sunday of the Year	Phil 1:20-24, 27
26th Sunday of the Year	Phil 2:1-11
27th Sunday of the Year	Phil 4:6-9
28th Sunday of the Year	Phil 4:12-14, 19-20
29th Sunday of the Year	1 Thes 1:1-5
30th Sunday of the Year	1 Thes 1:5-10
31st Sunday of the Year	1 Thes 2:7-9, 13
32nd Sunday of the Year	1 Thes 4:13-18
33rd Sunday of the Year	1 Thes 5:1-6
34th Sunday of the Year	1 Cor 15:20-26, 28
Trinity Sunday	2 Cor 13:11-13
Corpus Christi	1 Cor 10:16-17

Cycle B

1st Sunday of Advent	1 Cor 1:3-9
3rd Sunday of Advent	1 Thes 5:16-24
4th Sunday of Advent	Rom 16:25-27
Christmas	Ti 2:11-14
Christmas	Ti 3:4-7
Holy Family	Col 3:12-21
Octave of Christmas	Gal 4:4-7
2nd Sunday after Christmas	Eph 1:3-6, 15-18
Epiphany	Eph 3:2-3, 5-6
2nd Sunday of Lent	Rom 8:31-34
3rd Sunday of Lent	1 Cor 1:22-25
4th Sunday of Lent	Eph 2:4-10

Passion Sunday	Phil 2:6-11
Holy Thursday	1 Cor 11:23-26
Easter Vigil	Rom 6:3-11
Easter Sunday	1 Cor 5:6-8
Ascension	Eph 1:17-23
Pentecost Vigil	Rom 8:22-27
Pentecost Sunday	1 Cor 12:3-7, 12-13
2nd Sunday of the Year	1 Cor 6:13-15, 17-20
3rd Sunday of the Year	1 Cor 7:29-31
4th Sunday of the Year	1 Cor 7:32-35
5th Sunday of the Year	1 Cor 8:16-19, 22-23
6th Sunday of the Year	1 Cor 10:31, 11:1
7th Sunday of the Year	2 Cor 1:18-22
8th Sunday of the Year	2 Cor 3:1-6
9th Sunday of the Year	2 Cor 4:6-11
10th Sunday of the Year	2 Cor 4:13, 5:1
11th Sunday of the Year	2 Cor 5:6-10
12th Sunday of the Year	2 Cor 5:14-17
13th Sunday of the Year	2 Cor 8:7-9, 13-15
14th Sunday of the Year	2 Cor 12:7-10
15th Sunday of the Year	Eph 1:3-14
16th Sunday of the Year	Eph 2:13-18
17th Sunday of the Year	Eph 4:1-6
18th Sunday of the Year	Eph 4:17, 20-24
19th Sunday of the Year	Eph 4:30, 5:2
20th Sunday of the Year	Eph 5:15-20
21st Sunday of the Year	Eph 5:21-32
Trinity Sunday	Rom 8:14-17
Sacred Heart	Eph 3:8-12, 14-19

Cycle C

1st Sunday of Advent	1 Thes 3:12, 4:2
2nd Sunday of Advent	Phil 1:4-6, 8-11
3rd Sunday of Advent	Phil 4:4-7
Christmas	Ti 2:11-14
Christmas	Ti 3:4-7
Holy Family	Col 3:12-21
Octave of Christmas	Gal 4:4-7
2nd Sunday after Christmas	Eph 1:3-6, 15-18
Epiphany	Eph 3:2-3, 5-6
1st Sunday of Lent	Rom 10:8-13

2nd Sunday of Lent	Phil 3:17, 4:1
3rd Sunday of Lent	1 Cor 10:1-6, 10-12
4th Sunday of Lent	2 Cor 5:17-21
5th Sunday of Lent	Phil 3:8-14
Passion Sunday	Phil 2:6-11
Holy Thursday	1 Cor 11:23-26
Easter Vigil	Rom 6:3-11
Easter Sunday	1 Cor 5:6-8 or Col 3:1-4
Ascension	Eph 1:17-23
Pentecost Vigil	Rom 8:22-27
Pentecost Sunday	1 Cor 12:3-7, 12-13
2nd Sunday of the Year	1 Cor 12:4-11
3rd Sunday of the Year	1 Cor 12:12-30
4th Sunday of the Year	1 Cor 12:31, 13:13
5th Sunday of the Year	1 Cor 15:1-11
6th Sunday of the Year	1 Cor 15:12, 16:20
7th Sunday of the Year	1 Cor 15:45-49
8th Sunday of the Year	1 Cor 15:54-58
9th Sunday of the Year	Gal 1:1-2, 6-10
10th Sunday of the Year	Gal 1:11-19
11th Sunday of the Year	Gal 2:16, 19-21
12th Sunday of the Year	Gal 3:26-29
13th Sunday of the Year	Gal 5:1, 13-18
14th Sunday of the Year	Gal 6:14-18
15th Sunday of the Year	Col 1:15-20
16th Sunday of the Year	Col 1:24-28
17th Sunday of the Year	Col 2:12-14
18th Sunday of the Year	Col 3:1-5, 9-11
23rd Sunday of the Year	Phlm 9-10, 12-17
24th Sunday of the Year	1 Tm 1:12-17
25th Sunday of the Year	1 Tm 2:1-8
26th Sunday of the Year	1 Tm 6:11-16
27th Sunday of the Year	2 Tm 1:6-8, 13-14
28th Sunday of the Year	2 Tm 2:8-13
29th Sunday of the Year	2 Tm 3:14, 4:2
30th Sunday of the Year	2 Tm 4:6-8, 16-18
31st Sunday of the Year	2 Thes 1:11, 2:2
32nd Sunday of the Year	2 Thes 2:16, 3:5
33rd Sunday of the Year	2 Thes 3:7-12
34th Sunday of the Year	Col 1:12-20

For Further Reading

Amiot, Francios. *How to Read St. Paul.* New York: Paulist Press, 1966. A reflective summary of Paul's spirituality and teaching.

Bornkamm, Gunther. *Paul.* New York: Harper and Row, 1971. A deep, theological book on the life of Paul and the major themes in his letters.

Jerome Biblical Commentary. Englewood Cliffs, NJ: Prentice-Hall, 1967. Good articles by Joseph Fitzmyer on the "Life of Paul," "New Testament Epistles," and "Pauline Theology," plus commentaries by various authors on each of Paul's letters.

Johnson, Luke T. *Invitation to the New Testament Epistles III.* Garden City, NY: Doubleday, 1980. Simple commentaries on Paul's letters to the Colossians, Ephesians, to Timothy, and Titus.

LaVerdiere, Eugene A. *Invitation to the New Testament Epistles II.* Garden City, NY: Doubleday, 1980. Clear and simple commentaries on Paul's letters to the Thessalonians, Corinthians, Philippians, and to Philemon.

McKenzie, John L. *Light on the Epistles.* Chicago: Thomas More Press, 1975. A concise commentary on the letters of Paul and the other New Testament letters.

Norquist, Marilyn J. *How to Read and Pray St. Paul.* Liguori, MO: Liguori, 1979. A booklet containing a sketch of Paul's life and the main themes of his first seven letters. It also has some suggestions for family and group prayer.

Stanley, David M. *Boasting in the Lord.* New York: Paulist Press, 1973. A comprehensive study of the phenomenon of prayer in the letters of Paul.

Taylor, Michael J., ed. *A Companion to Paul.* New York: Alba House, 1975. A collection of scholarly articles useful for understanding Paul's theology.

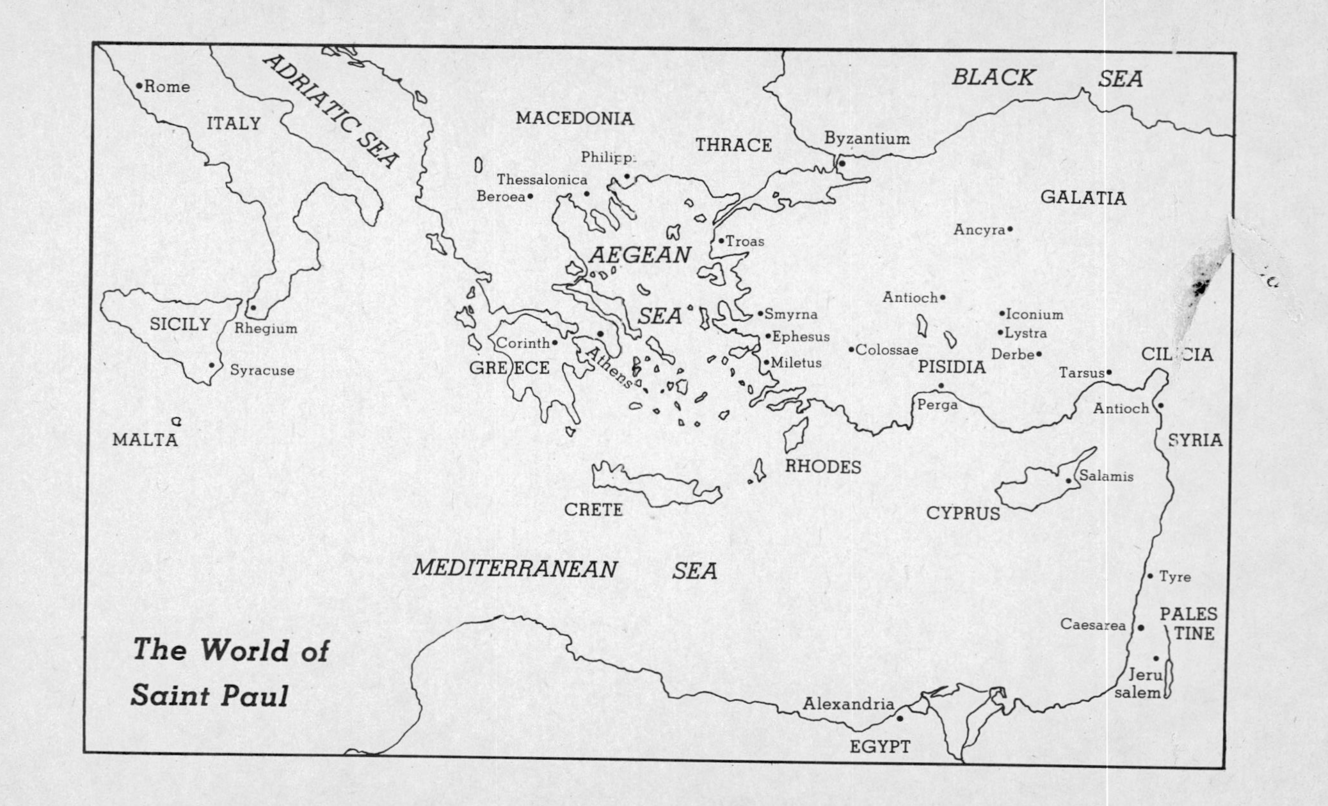

82 83 84 85 86 87 88 — S — 7 6 5 4 3 2 1